CAPACITY MEASUREMENT & IMPROVEMENT

CAPACITY MEASUREMENT & IMPROVEMENT

A Manager's Guide to Evaluating and Optimizing Capacity Productivity

THOMAS KLAMMER

IRWIN
Professional Publishing®
Chicago • London • Singapore

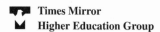 **Times Mirror**
Higher Education Group

Library of Congress Cataloging-in-Publication Data

Klammer, Thomas P., 1996
  Capacity measurement & improvement : a manager's guide to
evaluating and optimizing capacity productivity / Thomas Klammer.
    p. cm.
  Includes index.
  ISBN 0-7863-1066-9
  1. Industrial capacity—Measurement.   I. title.
HD69.C3k483   1997
658.5—dc20   96–19849

Printed in the United States of America

  3 4 5 6 7 8 9 0 BB 3 2 1 0 9 8 7 6

PREFACE

In a competitive economy, the effective use of capacity is critical. Unfortunately, there has been no universal approach to measuring the effectiveness of capacity use. The model explained in this primer provides this missing tool. The model helps us evaluate and change how our companies use and plan capacity.

Industry already uses a variety of capacity measures. However, there is often confusion about just what capacity means and how to describe capacity. Can anyone operate at 118 percent?

A recent discussion with six operating managers of a Fortune 500 company illustrates the problem. The dialogue focused on what kind of capacity use the company, as a whole, was experiencing. This simple exchange of ideas ended in a heated discussion. The six managers offered six different rates of the company's capacity productivity. Their estimates ranged from 20 percent to 110 percent. How could six managers from the same company have such different ideas about how the company was performing? This discussion shows differences in how management looks at plant capacity and its use.

Many questions arise when considering the total process of capacity management. Should we base plant capacity on the number of people working in the factory? Perhaps we should use the capacity of the installed equipment? Is wait time, due to an upstream constraint, an example of idle capacity, standby capacity, or waste? We can use or sell capacity, store it as inventory, or lose capacity when it is not used. How does your firm communicate these states of capacity?

Other issues also complicate the measurement of capacity use. Should we assign idle capacity to product cost? How can we give management insight into factory waste caused by design, planning, marketing, suppliers, and customers? The capacity model helps us answer these questions.

The idea of separating capacity into productive, nonproductive, and idle is the foundation of this model for evaluating capacity.

The model helps us provide information about these types of capacity and break each into subcomponents. It helps us evaluate existing capacity and to make future capacity decisions for hard and soft assets.

> *This economic model helps managers improve the productivity of existing capacity and significantly influences the capital investment decision process.*

The CAM-I Capacity Model is designed as an industry standard. The work of the CAM-I capacity group suggests that the model is conceptually sound. Several CAM-I companies have worked with the model and found it understandable and acceptable to both their business and operations teams. A primary purpose of this guide is to make the CAM-I Capacity Model widely known.

> *Product and market decisions must precede capacity decisions.*

ACKNOWLEDGMENTS

To operate successfully we must understand the capacity of our plants and production centers. This primer introduces the CAM-I Capacity Model. This is a process model that helps us communicate, evaluate, and use a variety of capacity measures.

The Cost Management Systems Program of the Consortium for Advanced Manufacturing—International (CAM-I) provided the environment to develop this primer. Since 1986, the Cost Management System (CMS) Program has given leading thinkers in industry, academia, and government a forum to challenge and improve cost management systems.

Without the support and structure of the CMS program this primer would not exist. Many ideas and concepts are the direct result of the cooperative efforts facilitated by the CMS program. This project received the support and encouragement of sponsor companies who recognize the need for continual improvement throughout their organizations. The CMS program acknowledges the extensive effort many individuals contributed to this project.

Edited and Revised by
Thomas Klammer
Regents Professor of Accounting
University of North Texas

Exhibits Created by
Alan Stratton
Dynamic Management Associates

EDS MCS Sales Support

A Joint Effort of
Gerry Brennan
Emerson Electric
Dan Callot
International Business Machines
Richard Davis
Valmet
Joe Donnelly (Chairman)
Arthur Andersen, LLP
Joe Edwards
Space Systems/Loral
Sheila Stafford
Eastman Chemical
Alan Stratton
Dynamic Management Associates
Alan Vercio
Texas Instruments

Useful contributions were also made by

Hank Adamany
Price Waterhouse
Dennis Daly
Metropolitan State University
Julian Freedman
Institute of Management Accountants
Judy Grewell
Electronic Data Systems
James Mackey
California State University Sacramento
Mike Roberts
RPM Group
Sandra Stirling
Texas Instruments
Peter A. Zampino
CAM-I
Consortium for Advanced Manufacturing–International

A project undertaken by the Consortium for Advanced Manufacturing–International Cost Management Systems Program
Arlington, Texas
CAM-I, 1995

TO THE READER

Capacity Measurement & Improvement provides a comprehensive communication tool, the CAM-I Capacity Model. This tool helps the operations team manage capacity more effectively. It gives management a better understanding of capacity. The model improves operations' ability to communicate capacity issues to management.

The primer provides a systematic analysis of capacity issues and includes several practical applications of the CAM-I Capacity Model. Throughout the primer, we use the terms *model* or *capacity model* when referring to the CAM-I Capacity Model.

The concepts of the capacity model come from work by H. L. Gantt, published in 1916, where he focused on identifying causes of variability and waste along with organizational responsibilities for capacity. The primer puts these ideas into the current organizational environment.

The primer uses illustrations, templates, and special icons for key points to summarize the capacity model ideas. The following icons are found throughout the text:

is used to highlight a Key Point

is used to highlight something Of Note

The term "CAM-I Capacity Model" is trademarked.

CONTENTS

INTRODUCTION

 Do management teams and operating teams understand capacity well enough to measure, communicate, and ultimately manage physical and people capacity processes effectively?

Welcome to the CAM-I Capacity Guide. The guide introduces the CAM-I Capacity Model and model templates that highlight capacity issues. The model provides a bridge between the language of operations, which is activities, and the language of management, which is finance. The model helps us show the processes, activities, and people who cause capacity use.

Capacity information is important. We already collect data about capacity and receive valuable capacity management information from the following types of measures:

- Output capacity measures—such as practical, theoretical, and scheduled—help us in annual planning, capital authorization, and inventory valuation.
- Tool capacity measures such as mean time between failures and RAM (reliability, availability, and maintainability) help us manage individual assets.

The capacity model gives us a process level tool that provides additional insight into capacity. Experience shows that a process capacity fog exists in many firms. This fog makes it difficult for operations to give management understandable capacity information.

Existing capacity measurements and management practices are important. However, often they do not provide enough insight into the amounts and sources of idle or nonproductive capacity. Does your firm identify different types of idle capacity? Does management know the cost of idle capacity? Who is responsible for variability or waste in the organization? What is the cost of nonproductive capacity?

Is this type of capacity information available to management in a language they use and understand? Often capacity management programs do not allow us to convert variability, cycle time, seconds, and other operational terms into financial data. Financial data is also important for supporting decisions to invest in capacity and products that use capacity.

> *Companies may lack insight into the amounts and sources of idle capacity. Companies may not communicate information about the capacity consumed by variability, waste, and other nonproductive capacity uses.*

The model allows operations to summarize capacity use for top management. It provides strategic information for business team decision making. The model allows us to drill down into the operating activities of the organization and provide capacity information about product costs, responsibility, and customers. It can help us communicate constraints.

The CAM-I Capacity Model is about communication. It makes many types of capacity visible and understandable for operating and management people. The model is a tool that can help firms compete more effectively. It helps lift the fog that surrounds existing capacity measures.

In our capacity journey we meet Pete and members of the operations team at the IMAC Company. Pete's difficulties in communicating information about capacity issues in IMAC's plants cause him to raise a series of questions about capacity. These are similar to the questions each of us consider as we strive to manage capacity more effectively. As we begin our journey, please keep a fundamental communication theme in mind.

> *You can't manage what you don't communicate.*
> *You can't communicate what you don't measure.*
> *You can't measure what you don't define.*
> *You can't define what you don't understand.*

1
CHAPTER

The IMAC Journey to Capacity Understanding Begins

Pete, the production manager of a modern IMAC company plant, shifts restlessly at his desk. He cannot quite shake the belief that as his plant embarks on a new opportunity, he is again going to have problems explaining the results to management. Pete sips coffee as he reviews the current situation.

Recently the IMAC Company invented Node-X, a product Pete's plant will manufacture using a Node-Matic machine. These machines are available in configurations with a range of output capabilities. IMAC's management decided to buy a high-volume machine. This machine gives IMAC extra capacity. Pete knows that management recognizes that existing Node-X demand does not require this much capacity. However, because the company fully loads product costs, the current measurement system makes him responsible for this unnecessary capacity cost.

SO MANY CAPACITY QUESTIONS

That evening Pete is restless. He keeps thinking about the Node-Matic machine and the Node-X capacity. Pete knows he can measure how the plant uses the Node-Matic, but can he communicate these

1

measurements to management? As Pete relaxes, he reflects on many questions concerning capacity and visualizes how these questions will affect IMAC (or any company).

What capacity measures do managers currently use?

Pete thinks, "Well, in production at IMAC we focus on scheduled capacity. This measure is what we use for our budget and it is the basis for assigning overhead costs to products. Scheduled capacity information helps us plan. I also know that marketing considers this product cost in the pricing formula. That is part of what is troublesome about the excess capacity of the Node-Matic equipment. I am not sure we communicate information about this type of capacity understandably. At planning meetings we do discuss the practical and theoretical capacity of the plant, particularly when we are considering making an additional investment in productive capacity. We have other measures of capacity, but these are the most important."

How much unused capacity exists?

"We have 40 percent unused for Node-X." Then Pete thinks about this answer. "What if I produce extra inventory for John's special project, or let Sheila make the shift changes she requested? Do I still have 40 percent excess capacity?"

How much unused capacity is assigned to product cost?

"We assign unused capacity cost to products at IMAC. However, when our competitors have less unused capacity it creates a problem. Suddenly the question becomes, can we compete? What is the effect of this excess capacity on the prices the marketing group quotes our customers?"

If a company produces the same output with different capacity, it almost certainly has a different cost.

EXHIBIT 1

Same Output—Different Capacity—Different Cost?

High Cost Co   Low Cost Co

Is all idle capacity the same?

"Many types of idle capacity exist. At another company we discussed the idea that idle capacity can be marketable, but some is not marketable. We also identified off-limits capacity. There may be other classifications."

Does IMAC have the right information about various types of capacity?

"I think we do in the plant. However, management may not get good information on all types of capacity. I would like a better way to give information to management about the effects of various activities and decisions on IMAC's plant capacity."

Could IMAC suddenly discover a high percentage of idle or unsalable capacity?

"Within operations we know this capacity did not suddenly become idle or unsalable. At IMAC we have many internal financial and operating reports. I hope these reports identify this idle or unsalable capacity before it is a serious business threat." After a pause, Pete reflects, "We did have this type of situation at another production facility recently. This cost was hidden from management."

Who, besides the manufacturing team, is responsible for capacity usage?

"At IMAC this is an extensive list. Marketing, product development, quality, accounting, training, human resources, facilities, customers, and suppliers each have an impact. They all influence the types of capacity we acquire. They also influence how we use capacity. This raises additional capacity questions that a better process tool would help us answer. The questions include these:

- "Does marketing know the impact of a special customer request or the effect of the variability in their demands for products?
- "Does the accounting team know how their product costing or capital justification procedures influence capacity acquisitions and usage?
- "Does the human resource team understand the influences that people issues have on capacity?
- "Do we know how much capacity is the responsibility of other teams?
- "Does an agenda for capacity improvement exist for each group?

EXHIBIT 2

Who is Responsible?

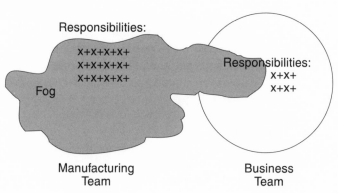

Responsibilities:

X+X+X+X+
X+X+X+X+
X+X+X+X+

Fog

Responsibilities:
X+X+
X+X+

Manufacturing
Team

Business
Team

At IMAC the answer to several of these questions may be no! These are important issues that may help us improve our capacity productivity."

> *A better understanding and communication of capacity information helps us understand which teams or functions are really responsible for this capacity and its use.*

Despite this assertion, there are still more questions about capacity.

Can IMAC measure the capacity impact of their improvement programs?

Pete considers the recent initiatives at IMAC. "We have business reports that do not seem to reflect the improvements that operating people feel exist. Can we (and do we) measure the individual or combined results that our JIT, KANBAN, TPM (total productive maintenance), standardization, and training programs have on capacity? Management needs this understanding when evaluating these initiatives." Exhibit 3 illustrates why we need to understand capacity effects.

EXHIBIT 3

Combined Results

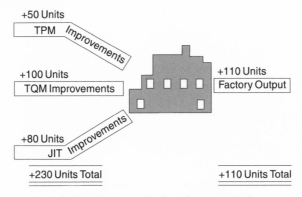

What happened to the other 120 units?

Do our inventory strategies allow us to get the best use of our available capacity?

"As a production manager, I realize that any Node-Matic capacity that I do not use to support current sales or build inventory is lost capacity. I can only store capacity as inventory. That is one reason we measure the full cost of production. However, what if the cost of storing inventory changes? What are the value-added changes in the product line? Should this lead to changes in our policies for stored capacity (inventory creation)? We may be insensitive to these issues and the demands of different product strategies. We do not have a capacity reporting system that captures the effects of these activities."

How do we convert manufacturing activities into a common language for operations and management?

"This is a key question. (See Exhibit 4.) Making the trade-offs between diverse activities on the factory floor is sometimes quite simple, particularly in a small or focused factory. For instance, with the Node-X production facility the business team and I can easily work out the capacity issues these questions raise. Even here, most of the measures must be in dollars. Scheduling production with John, my marketing manager, is easier when I show him how much expediting an order costs. Many companies, including ours, have factories that are large and complex. Trade-offs in these environments require us to use a common language. Usually this is money, the language of finance and management."

How much reserve capacity or buffer does the company need? Who is responsible for this buffer?

"At IMAC we face a dilemma. If we have buffer inventory, we can make quick commitments to our customers. However, as the buffers go higher, so do costs. We may not know how much of a buffer we need. Who is responsible? Everyone has responsibility. As production manager, I am responsible for part of this buffer. So are the suppliers, customers, and members of the business team. Our problem is, we do not say how much of this responsibility rests with each group. Perhaps we do not fully understand the critical balance between customer commitment and cost."

EXHIBIT 4

Translating Time into Dollars

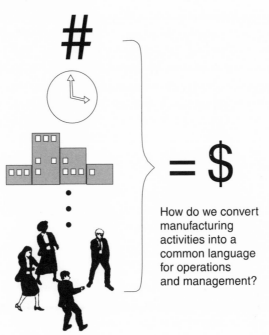

How do we convert
manufacturing
activities into a
common language
for operations
and management?

EXHIBIT 5

The Dilemma

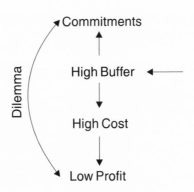

Can IMAC create additional capacity without additional capital investment?

"It is quite possible. Just the other day, a vice president and the controller were discussing the high cost of adding capacity. Meanwhile, my plant has idle capacity. I guess these are more questions for my list."

Finally, Pete drifts off to sleep. The next morning Pete quickly prepares a list of capacity questions.

Unanswered Capacity Questions

What capacity measures are in use?

How much unused capacity exists?

How much unused capacity is assigned to product cost?

Is all idle capacity the same?

Does the right information about the various types of capacity exist?

Could we suddenly discover a high percentage of idle or unsalable capacity?

Who, besides the manufacturing team, is responsible for capacity usage?

   ✓ Does marketing know the impact of a special customer request or the impact of the variability in their demands for products?

   ✓ Does the accounting team know how their product costing or capital justification procedures affect capacity acquisitions and usage?

   ✓ Does the human resource team understand the influence that people issues have on capacity?

   ✓ Do we know how much capacity is the responsibility of other teams?

   ✓ Does an agenda for capacity improvement exist for each group?

Can we measure the capacity impact of our improvement programs?

Do our inventory strategies allow us to get the best use of our available capacity?

How do we convert manufacturing activities into a common language for operations and management?

How much reserve capacity or buffer does the company need? Who is responsible for this buffer?

How can we create additional capacity without additional capital investment?

IMAC'S SEARCH FOR CAPACITY ANSWERS CONTINUES

Pete asked the operating team to study ways to communicate better information about how the Node-Matic plant used capacity. To get the team started, Pete provided his list of unanswered questions.

> *If your company has good answers to each or most of these questions, it is fortunate. If opportunities for improvement exist in capacity management, application of the CAM-I Capacity Model should be useful.*

Pete's team began their study by looking up the definition of capacity. They knew immediately that this was only the start of developing a process model for showing the activities that influenced capacity in the IMAC environment.

Capacity **1.** the ability to contain, absorb, or receive and hold **2.** *a)* the amount of space that can be filled; room for holding; content or volume [a tank with a *capacity* of 21 gallons] *b)* the point at which no more can be contained [filled to *capacity*] **3.** the power of receiving and holding knowledge, impressions, etc.; mental ability **4.** the ability or qualifications (*for*, or *to* do, something); aptitude **5.** maximum output or producing ability [operating at *capacity*] **6.** the quality of being adapted (*for* something) or susceptible (*of* something); capability; potentiality **7.** a condition of being qualified or authorized; position, function, status, etc. [acting in the *capacity* of an advisor] **8.** *Elec. same as* CAPACITANCE. **9.** *Law* legal authority or competency — **SYN.** see FUNCTION

Webster's New World Dictionary—Third College Edition

The IMAC team looked at the different types of capacity. Once these types were identified, they felt they could measure each type and devise appropriate ways to help express to management this use of capacity.

First, Pete and the team needed to define maximum capacity. To help identify this critical measure, they read publications that addressed capacity. Few provided a comprehensive explanation they could use. The most useful definitions were in several writings from the early 1900s, particularly those by H. L. Gantt.

> **Two of these articles are found in Appendixes A and B.**

In measuring maximum capacity, one major source of difficulty was that IMAC used varying production rates to produce different products from the same process. IMAC can make 20 of some products in an hour, while others zip through at 200 in an hour. When the process involves a batch operation, the rate sometimes depends on the size or fullness of the batch. The team examined various measures in its search for a common element to measure maximum capacity.

Eventually they found the common element—**time.** Most capacity rates are expressions of output per unit of time. For example, the Node-Matic schedule might be for 500 Node-X units per hour. An accounts payable clerk might process 60 invoices an hour.

> **The common element of capacity is time.**

The team struggled to understand how to use the time idea as a communication device. Finally, someone suggested looking at the input of the operation. Another team member observed, "We can state all capacity measures in a common form: available time." An accounts payable clerk is available 8 hours a day. A machine is available 24 hours a day. We can convert all output rates into a time measurement. Time is the common denominator. The key is to ask, How do we use the available time?

A remaining task was to find terms that everyone in the company would understand. The common measure that did not incorporate any other bias was the **total time available.** As shown in Exhibit 6, total time available is 24 hours per day, 7 days per week, 365 days per year (168 hours per week or 8,760 hours per year). The exact form of expression is not critical. Once the team agreed on a definition for maximum capacity, they sensed that other definitions would be easier.

Production people, such as Pete and the operations team, regularly discuss capacity. However, capacity involves more than the equipment. It includes the existing facility, the people to operate and support production, and material availability. The team needed a

EXHIBIT 6

Time Available

24 Hours/Day
730 Hours/Month
8760 Hours/Year

tool that could communicate information about different capacity-related activities. The team decided they could show the influences of these types of capacity separately or together.

The team already had many time metrics on capacity use. For example, IMAC measures labor hours, machine run time, and setup time. The team also felt they could easily get or estimate the other measures they would need.

It was easy to decide that as time passed capacity was used or capacity was not used. Pete's team reasoned that all further capacity definitions were subsets of *used capacity* or *idle capacity.*

In an ideal environment, a company would use all capacity in production. IMAC would make good product for sale. A good product is the right product, at the right quality, at the right time, for the right customer. Any deviation from this standard consumes capacity, but is less desirable than the production of a good product. However, there are reasons a plant or a production center might not produce a good product. Setups and maintenance use capacity but a good product is not a direct result of this capacity use. Used capacity should be classified as either *productive* or *nonproductive.*

 Time available is either used or idle. Time used is either productive or nonproductive.

At this point, Judy, a member of the IMAC team, visited a CAM-I meeting and heard a presentation on the CAM-I Capacity Model. She brought the model back to the team.

2
CHAPTER

The Model

The model is a multiple-part communication tool that helps us define and use capacity measures. The model adds insight that helps us address many capacity questions at all organizational levels. It is the economic mirror that operations needs to give management information about business operations (the processes).

The model provides summary information for top management and strategic information for business team decision making. By drilling down into the operating activities we can describe capacity information related to product costs and responsibility. We can use the model with forecasting tools and for historical comparisons. The model will also interface with dynamic capacity modeling and simulation tools.

Judy comments to the IMAC work team: "The efforts of the CAM-I capacity work group illustrate there are many uses of the model. As we review the model, we will see why it has value for IMAC. After our discussion of the Node-Matic plant capacity, it was exciting to find others struggling with the same issues. The summary model, which we examine first, is important in a production facility with excess capacity."

The CAM-I Capacity Model is first and foremost a communication tool. The capacity work team determined that the use of color or a background shading for different types of capacity made the message more powerful. Green became the color associated with productive capacity, red the color associated with nonproductive capacity, and yellow the color associated with idle capacity. The text includes references to these colors as well as the capacity type as a reminder of the importance of a unique visual communication when using the tool. Because we still often communicate in black and white rather than color, we use the following background coding in our exhibits as an alternative to the color itself. Idle capacity is shown with a background of gray and nonproductive capacity with a background of black. Productive capacity is shown with a white background.

THE SUMMARY MODEL

The model illustrated in Exhibit 7 suggests that any company can subdivide total or rated capacity into: idle, nonproductive, and productive capacity. This summary template helps us answer this question: *If we had 10 minutes to present the state of capacity to the board of directors, what template would we use?*

The power of the model as a communication tool improves when we visually code the three major capacity groupings. Color or distinctive backgrounds highlight each type of capacity. We code the productive capacity as white (green), the idle capacity as gray (yellow), and the nonproductive capacity as black (red). These visual codes ease communication and send strong signals to top management and the rest of the organization. It becomes obvious what portion of our capacity fits into each category. Below is a brief explanation of these capacity codes.

Nonproductive capacity may be necessary under existing conditions, but it is an undesirable use of capacity in an ideal situation.

EXHIBIT 7

The Summary Capacity Model

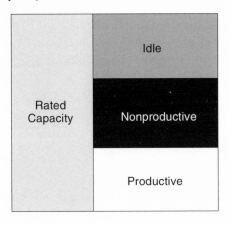

The black color for nonproductive capacity is a warning signal. The message of the black box is this: "Black capacity is the portion of our time and money that results in capacity use, but not good products." This capacity offers an opportunity for improvement. We try to eliminate the variability, waste, and other nonproductive activities and seek to decrease the percentage of nonproductive capacity. A primary purpose of the capacity model is to highlight and show the level of nonproductive activity.

Idle capacity may exist for many reasons. It may offer the company opportunities. At other times, production center capacity remains idle for strategic or legal reasons. The message of the gray box, particularly for management and business teams, is this: "Gray shows how much existing capacity is idle and offers an opportunity to grow the business or change policies that create this capacity." This capacity is an opportunity for the business team to convert idle capacity to productive capacity, or to abandon capacity.

Productive capacity use is desirable. It provides value to the customer and results in the production of good products or services. We want to have more productive capacity. The white coding is an indicator of our existing or target level of productive capacity. As shown in "Pieces of the Capacity Model," each summary category has several parts:

PIECES OF THE CAPACITY MODEL

Rated Capacity = Idle + Nonproductive + Productive Capacity

- *Rated capacity* uses a time measure. It assumes 24 hours a day, every day, with each tool producing at benchmark rates. The cost of this capacity is 100 percent of the total cost assignable to the process.

- *Idle capacity* includes marketable, not marketable, and off-limits capacity.
  - *Idle marketable:* a market exists but capacity is idle because of competitor market share, product substitutes, distribution constraints, or price/cost constraints. This capacity is the responsibility of the business team.
  - *Idle not marketable:* a market does not exist or management decides not to participate in the market. This capacity is a target for abandonment.
  - *Idle off-limits:* capacity unavailable because of holidays, contracts, or management policies or strategies. It remains off-limits until management decides it is marketable.

- *Nonproductive capacity* is capacity not in a productive state or in one of the defined idle states. Nonproductive capacity subsets include these: setups, standby, scheduled downtime, unscheduled downtime, rework, and scrap. The model helps us provide data about each type of nonproductive capacity.
  - *Standby* is nonproductive because of variability caused by suppliers, customers, or internal operations. Standby is a capacity buffer that helps the firm deal with this variability. Standby results from waiting or because a particular operation has more capacity than the factory constraint.
  - *Waste* may be scrap, rework, and yield loss. Waste comes from multiple sources.
  - *Setups and maintenance* may occur for various reasons, but all make the resource nonproductive.

- *Productive capacity* is capacity used to change the product or provide the service. Productive use of capacity provides tangible changes in the product or service that are of value to the customer. Examples include cutting, molding, welding, painting, furnace time, and assembly. Productive capacity results in the production of good products. It may also represent the use of capacity for process or product development.

THE CAM-I CAPACITY MODEL

Judy summarizes the full CAM-I Capacity Model, shown in Exhibit 8, for the team: "The model drills down from the total rated capacity to more specific capacity subparts. Color or other coding helps us provide information about the states of capacity. The model provides a standard format that helps everyone understand the activities that use capacity. For example, Pete, you can see how the model

EXHIBIT 8

The Full Capacity Model

Rated Capacity	Summary Model	Industry-Specific Model	Strategy-Specific Model	Traditional Model
Rated Capacity	Idle	Not marketable	Excess Not Usable	Theoretical
		Off-limits	Management Policy	
			Contractual	
			Legal	
		Marketable	Idle But Usable	Practical
	Non-productive	Standby	Process Balance	Scheduled
			Variability	
			Scrap	
		Waste	Rework	
			Yield Loss	
		Maintenance	Scheduled	
			Unscheduled	
			Time	
		Setups	Volume	
			Changeover	
	Productive	Process Development		
		Product Development		
		Good Products		

highlights the large percentage of initial idle capacity that management built into our Node-X plant. This is an opportunity for the business team to grow our productive capacity."

The summary capacity model we discussed earlier (see Exhibit 7) is incorporated as columns one and two of the full model shown in Exhibit 8. These columns provide the general state of capacity in a form that is useful for decision makers. We could provide this information for the entire firm, a plant, a process, a production center, a machine, or an individual.

The third and fourth columns of the model allow us to provide a comprehensive analysis of various states of capacity. The general capacity categories listed in these columns in the general comprehensive model appear to be reasonably standard. However, as a specific industry applies this model, the specific subcategories may vary. We may find that there are industry-specific groupings of nonproductive capacity. The detailed specification of the types of capacity is particularly useful for business and operating teams focusing on using capacity more effectively. Later we review a series of time and economic templates on strategy, responsibility, and product costing. Each template uses the details found in the capacity model.

Judy continues to review the model for the IMAC team. "We expect differences in the types and quantity of idle, nonproductive, and productive capacity based on industry or strategic factors. For example, our Node-Matic line produces only a single product so setups cause little nonproductive capacity. Other IMAC factories produce hundreds of different products and require more time for setups. By using industry specific or strategy specific templates, we can focus on the common and distinctive features of capacity. This gives us benchmarking opportunities inside and outside the company."

The final column represents the traditional capacity reporting measures that most firms use for planning and scheduling. This articulation allows us to tie elements of the general model to traditional reporting systems. This column allows us to avoid developing a new set of measurement tools. Instead we can translate traditional information into a new format.

Pete suggests that reviewing the basic model objectives and the characteristics of this tool might be useful.

OBJECTIVE—BRIDGE THE GAP

The model as shown in Exhibit 9 helps us convert operating information into the financial information. The language of operations is time, units, pounds, and throughput. The language of management is profit from operations and cash flow. Without adequate communication, resource allocation decisions are arbitrary.

Kaoru Ishikawa, author of *What Is Total Quality Control? The Japanese Way*, tells us to align operating measurements of quality with financial measurements:

> There can be no quality control which ignores price, profit, and cost control. Insufficient supply of a product which is in demand will inconvenience customers. An excessive supply will be a waste of labor, raw materials, and energy. Cost control and quality control are two sides of the same coin. To engage in effective cost control, effective quality control must be implemented. One must always strive to supply a product with just quality, just price, and just amount.[1]

The primary business process measures are cost, time, and quality. Trade-offs among these metrics are comparable only when we use the common language of management—money. Financial comparisons consider costs and revenues, now and in the future. The tool kit of business continues to expand. Activity-based costing,

EXHIBIT 9

The Bridge

Bridge the communication gap	
Operations:	Management:
• Time	• Profit
• Units	• Cash flow
• Pounds	
• Throughput	

Since 1986, CAM-I has taken a leadership role in developing and publicizing new cost management tools. CAM-I has been particularly active with activity-based costing and activity-based management methodology development and technology transfer.

target costing, cost of quality, investment management, and other techniques supplement our traditional planning and control tools. The capacity model is another valuable tool we can use.

Alexander Church in 1915 and H. L. Gantt in 1916, both operations experts, discussed the importance of bridging the gap between operational and financial language (see Exhibit 9). It is as relevant today as it was then.

> Another cause of trouble is that the design of a cost system may be approached from two opposite view points—that of the commercial accountant, who thinks in ledger accounts and that of the shop staff, who think in terms of hours, men and materials. The accountant thinks of detail as troublesome necessity: the shop staff knows that the detail is the lifeblood of a cost system.[2]
>
> Most of the cost systems in use, and the theories on which they are based, have been devised by accountants for the benefit of financiers, whose aim has been to criticize the factory and to make it responsible for all the shortcomings of the business. In this they have succeeded admirably, largely because the methods used are not so devised as to enable the superintendent to present his side of the case.[3]

The core of the capacity model applications is information we can express (or translate) using both time and dollars. The model is a collection of capacity data that includes the **supply of capacity** and the **demand for capacity**. We might measure the capacity of available production centers. Judy illustrates this point: "Here at IMAC we could focus on the Node-Matic machine at one level. We could consider all the machines the company owns at another level."

Time is the common denominator and is part of the raw data needed to build the **basic economic template.** A time template is usually more valuable at operating levels of the organization. For management an economic template with financial measurements is more useful. Using raw time data, we can build the economic template by adding process cost and reconstructing the model. As shown in Exhibit 10, this helps business and manufacturing meet. See Chapter 3 for a more complete illustration.

Pete and the IMAC team see specific applications for the model. Measuring the amount of idle capacity associated with Node-X production, in time and in dollars, will reduce the risks for both operations and management. It will make it easier to see the potential conflict between normal performance measurement models and the decision to have excess capacity. It helps show responsibility for costs more effectively. Pete believes the model also makes us less likely to fall into the trap of initially trying to recover total product costs. We know part of these costs exist for strategic reasons.

CHARACTERISTICS OF THE MODEL

The model is more than a valuable link between operations and management. Consider the characteristics, summarized on the next page, before examining the details of the full model.

EXHIBIT 10

The Teams

A common language brings the teams together.

CAPACITY MODEL CHARACTERISTICS

Financial and Operational Integration. The capacity model starts with operational data and assembles it in a form that allows operations to communicate the economic effects of capacity decisions.

Closed loop. The model uses all available time and reports all capacity somewhere. If there is a productivity improvement, the model shows where the capacity went. All the cost of the process is traced and assigned to categories of capacity.

Focus on idle capacity. The model shows different types of idle capacity. This focuses attention on opportunities to manage idle capacity.

Focus on nonproductive activities. The model specifically captures all nonproductive uses of capacity. Making nonproductive capacity visible is a critical contribution of the capacity model.

Process/activity based. The capacity model focuses on process and the activities that make up the process. It adds value to existing production centers and performance capacity measures within the context of the overall process.

Responsibility reporting. The capacity model allows more effective assignment of responsibility, particularly for idle and nonproductive capacity.

Industry standard. The model allows companies to use an established general approach to capacity measurement. It facilitates comparisons and benchmarking.

Financial and Operational Integration

Managing with both financial and operational data is important and can provide a competitive advantage. Using an integrated approach, we can show the positive financial improvement that comes from making an operational improvement. Often tracing operational improvements to the bottom line is difficult. In addition, financially justified improvements often do not result in operational improvement.

The model addresses this integration in several ways. The basis of the model is the operational data used to manage the factory. At IMAC, Pete's team can focus on how long they use the Node-Matic machine to produce the number of Node-X's marketing requires. They can give marketing cost information about this use of capacity. This is quite different from financial models that begin with the chart of account classifications.

We assemble capacity data in a process format. This allows us to apply business process management. Our business teams have better process understanding. For instance, we now know the cost of setups, standby process capacity, and the idle capacity we choose not to use. Activity costing techniques help bring relevant financial data to process management.

We can probably manage operations effectively without an economic mirror. However, financial data also often represents a more powerful mode of communication for operating people than seconds, pounds, or movements. For example, we might show that each movement of materials costs the company $30 and affects the money available for profit sharing. This approach may get more action than a request for suggestions to reduce the number of materials moves.

Having an economic mirror is critical in communications from manufacturing to management. Pete knows that telling senior management, "the new combination of lead time and cycle time policies add 200 setups a week and reduce process yields in manufacturing" may not get their attention. However, if his message says, "these additional setups consume $40,000 worth of capacity a week and result in a process yield instability worth an additional $10,000 a week," the message is more useful. Surfacing the $2.6 million annual impact of the lead time and cycle time policies may cause management to reconsider their decision. Alternatively, the additional revenue generated by the shorter lead times, or management's belief that the manufacturing team can reduce setup time and improve process stability may warrant the policy changes.

Finance is the language of management. Providing operational driven financial information is a major service to companies.

Closed Loop

The model is a closed loop (see Exhibit 11) that integrates the time and economic capacity reporting systems. The model is all inclusive. We use 24 hours a day, 365 days a year as the basis for all measurements. Each process (production center or work bench) reports in this format. If we make a productivity improvement in a process, the model reports where the freed up capacity went. If the improvement is made in a constraint, there is more output capability. If the improvement is made in a nonconstraint, additional capacity in process balance is created.

Traditional capacity measures focus on budget or practical capacity. As budgeted capacity increases, the unit cost usually declines. However, these measures do not focus attention on the cost of having extra capacity available. Under the capacity model, if the demand for Node-X increases, Pete's plant would show more productive and less idle capacity. Closed loop information is quite different from information shown by traditional measures. For example, IMAC's traditional measures focus on assigning the full cost, based on today's production, to the product. This cost is assigned despite the impact of this policy on performance measures and without considering the reason the idle capacity was created.

Focus on Idle Capacity

Information on the amount and cost of idle capacity is critical. If a company has too much idle capacity, it may be unable to compete due to high cost. If a company is experiencing capacity constraints,

EXHIBIT 11

The Closed Loop

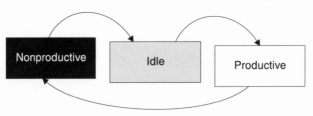

Capacity responsibility is contained in a closed loop.

it may be unable to take advantage of opportunities. Traditional measures do not provide either management or operating personnel with significant useful information about the amount and cost of idle capacity.

> *Understanding the sources of idle capacity helps the business team create more productive capacity.*

In the IMAC situation, management made a strategic decision to invest in excess Node-Matic capacity. Before deciding, did they adequately consider the cost of this extra capacity? Was this cost part of the investment management model? Explicit information on the idle capacity cost would give management the incentive to make this idle capacity productive.

Focus on Nonproductive Activities

The model ensures that, in total, we capture and report all the nonproductive use of capacity. The identification of nonproductive capacity helps operating teams prioritize process improvements that reduce nonproductive activities.

> *A critical element of the capacity model is the focus on sources and cost of nonproductive capacity.*

According to Gantt, nonproductive capacity is the place to begin working productivity improvements.

> [Gantt] was convinced that a study of idleness is much more effective in increasing the output of the plant than the study of what has been called 'efficiency,' and that the one should always be completed before the other was attempted.

Adding capacity is an easy, but expensive, way to solve a perceived capacity shortage. Good insight into nonproductive activities highlights opportunities to convert nonproductive to productive capacity and avoid capital investment.

Process/Activity Based

 | **The model is a process model.**

Capacity is a primary characteristic of a process. Another characteristic is activity. An analysis of activities will help us present the state of capacity at a point in time. Activity management has grown rapidly since the early 1980s. Now we find companies focus on business process management, activity-based management, and value engineering. The capacity model (see Exhibit 12) is an aggregate of activities for a process or series of processes. We can apply the model to processes such as product development. We can apply it to support processes, such as procurement, or service processes, such as the cafeteria.

As a process measure, the model complements and adds value to existing tool and performance capacity measures. Tool measures focus on the state or substate of increments of capacity at any time. Examples of production center states are these: non-scheduled, standby, downtime, and productive. Production center performance measures address the quality of the productive time and account for yield loss and speed loss of the equipment. Process measures identify production center activities in relation to the entire process.

EXHIBIT 12

The Process Model

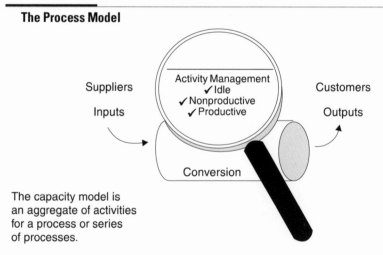

The capacity model is
an aggregate of activities
for a process or series
of processes.

These include standby caused by factory imbalance or processing material that we later scrap.

Below is a comparison of the CAM-I measurement methodology and two current measures of equipment productivity.

MEASUREMENT METHODOLOGY

Area of Measurement Focus	RAM	OEE	CAM-I
Time States	x	x	x
Equipment Performance		x	x
Process Performance			x

RAM = Reliability Availability Maintainability
OEE = Overall Equipment Effectiveness

Responsibility Reporting

With activities as the building blocks of the capacity model, assigning responsibility is easier. This assignment is critical in communicating opportunities for improvement, and it requires a transition from the traditional view that the manufacturing team has total responsibility for factory output. We can track the effects of the many teams that have a direct influence on the factory. Responsible teams include these: the business team, the manufacturing team, and support teams that influence capacity productivity.

The capacity model helps Pete's IMAC team specifically show that responsibility for initial idle capacity rests with top management. It also highlights the responsibility of marketing to find customers who can profitably fill this idle Node-Matic capacity. If the product development people use existing capacity, the model will focus on the time and cost of this use of productive capacity.

Industry Standard

Standards, when appropriately applied, can provide valuable insight and aid resource allocation. Knowing that $700,000 of nonproductive activities exist in a manufacturing process is important.

Knowing that a similar set of nonproductive activities exists in nine other factories could be a competitive advantage. With this information we may justify a process improvement that does not make sense on an individual plant basis. For example, suppose we could save $500,000 in nonproductive setup cost by investing in an $800,000 training program. For a single plant this is not a good investment. Suppose we can use the training program in seven other plants, at a cost of $200,000 a plant. Now the investment makes sense.

The CAM-I Capacity Model was developed to provide an industry standard. As a standard the model provides:

- A communication tool that uses the language of both operations teams and business teams.
- Benchmarks in common denominators of time, money, and responsibility.
- Drill down capabilities.
- A common documentation format.
- A technique for communicating with suppliers and customers.
- A reduction in the "not invented here" problem.
- A tool for benchmarking capacity management processes.

Judy finishes going over the model characteristics for the IMAC operating team and Pete suggests that the team next carefully consider idle, nonproductive, and productive capacity.

 The CAM-I Capacity Model is an industry standard.

IDLE CAPACITY

Does your business team know how much idle capacity exists? Can they explain the reasons for this idle capacity? Traditional measurements do little to highlight idle capacity. They provide even less information on the types and reasons for this idle capacity. **Communicating idle capacity information is one priority of the capacity model.**

EXHIBIT 13

Idle Capacity

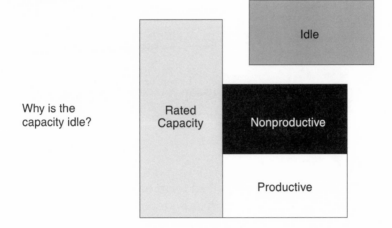

Pete and his IMAC team knew they had a significant amount of idle capacity (see Exhibit 13). This knowledge started them on their capacity journey. When the team examined the Node-Matic idle capacity, using the 24-hour time measure, they could identify several types of idle capacity. Idle capacity existed because the Node-Matic plant could make more product than IMAC could currently sell. Sometimes, the team ran the Node-Matic machine at a slower rate because of the slack demand. Even this is a form of idle capacity.

Types of Idle Capacity

A critical step is communicating information about the types of idle capacity. The model in Exhibit 14 identifies three general types of idle capacity: **marketable**, unused but usable; **not marketable**, unused and not usable; and **off-limits**, unused and not usable.

Idle marketable capacity is where a market exists but our capacity is idle. Reasons may include competitors' market share, the existence of product substitutes, distribution constraints, or price/cost constraints. The business team, not the operating team, has direct responsibility for capacity the company could use, but is currently unable to use.

EXHIBIT 14

The CAM-I Capacity Model

Rated Capacity	Summary Model	Industry-Specific Model	Strategy-Specific Model	Traditional Model
		Not Marketable	Excess Not Usable	
	Idle	Off-Limits	Management Policy	Theoretical
			Contractual	
			Legal	
		Marketable	Idle but Usable	Practical
Rated Capacity		Process Balance		

Slowdown can be a disguised form of idle capacity. The slowing of a production center or process step may occur when idle but marketable capacity exists.

Giving visibility to idle but marketable capacity is important. Assume that a distribution problem causes the production level of a factory to fall. The capacity model highlights the amount of idle capacity that is available, but not used because of the distribution problem. This focuses management attention on the problem.

A traditional measurement system does not provide this information. Instead, the increased cost per unit, because of the lower sales, becomes part of inventory cost. Often this becomes the assumed responsibility of operations. Additional illustrations of how the capacity model highlights responsibility are found in Chapter 3.

 | *Idle marketable capacity is determined by the process constraint.*

Idle not-marketable capacity is where a market does not exist or management made a strategic decision to no longer participate in the market. Capacity classified as not marketable is a target for abandonment. Sometimes the not-marketable capacity is the result of obsolescence. Currently not-marketable capacity may become marketable with an upgrade or retrofit.

Because alternatives range from abandonment to additional investment, how we express key information about not-marketable capacity may be critical. Business teams need information on the types and quantity of this capacity. Information on the cost of any additional investments needed to make the capacity marketable must be available. The implications of an abandonment decision should be part of the communication. Your company probably already collects this information as part of the capital investment management process.

Idle off-limits capacity is unavailable for use. Examples of this capacity include government regulations, management policy, and contractual arrangements. Capacity held for strategic growth is off-limits until management decides it should qualify as marketable.

> *Idle off-limits includes capacity held for strategic growth.*

Regulations or legal requirements may be a major reason for idle capacity. Sometimes laws prohibit work on certain holidays. Environmental restrictions may limit how much a plant may work. Often management has only limited ability to change the level of this idle capacity. The costs associated with this capacity are necessary if a company is to operate in a particular industry or location.

Off-limits capacity also comes from constraints created by management policy. A company's management may decide not to work certain shifts or holidays. Contractual agreements may restrict capacity use. This capacity becomes marketable when management decides to change existing policy. If we add a third factory shift, less idle off-limits capacity exists. The model helps give the business team information that can help it manage idle capacity.

A particular type of idle capacity may appear in several categories. If the EPA prohibits production of pollutants during rush hour traffic, this capacity is off-limits. If the EPA limits pollutants to a certain amount, any excess capacity in the plant is not marketable. This excess capacity provides an opportunity for abandonment. If we cannot use it, why keep it? We may also consider the capacity as

EXHIBIT 15

Forms of Idle Capacity

nonproductive. It may represent an opportunity for reengineering. Are there investments the company can make that will reduce pollutants and make more of the existing capacity usable?

As shown in Exhibit 15, it may result from overinvestment in physical or people resources. It may appear because of restructuring or downsizing decisions. Idle capacity may also result from productivity or continuous improvement initiatives, including the adoption of JIT or activity accounting. Information about idle capacity is particularly helpful in making product capacity mix decisions and in the capital authorization process. A major focus of the model is to provide information that will help the business team formulate an appropriate management strategy.

Pete could see how the new visibility of idle capacity would help his team suggest changes in the IMAC decision-making models.

NONPRODUCTIVE CAPACITY

Nonproductive capacity is capacity that is neither in a productive state nor in one of the defined idle states (see Exhibit 16). Nonproductive capacity includes setups, maintenance, standby, scheduled downtime, unscheduled downtime, rework, and scrap. Variability is a primary cause of nonproductive capacity. The model shown in Exhibit 15 provides a standard form for communicating information on each type of nonproductive capacity use.

EXHIBIT 16

Nonproductive Capacity

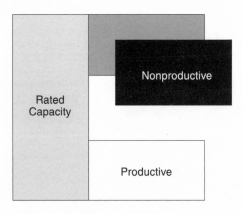

Why is the capacity nonproductive?

All companies have nonproductive capacity. However, traditional companywide capacity reports do not focus on nonproductive uses of capacity. They report practical and scheduled capacity. These capacity measures are useful for product planning and committing to customers, but they do not expose process waste or variability. A major objective of the capacity model is to provide information on waste and variability.

We can segregate nonproductive capacity in many ways. A common way is to use the value chain—suppliers, ourselves, and customers. Each causes variability and waste that increase nonproductive capacity.

Pete and the IMAC team knew that as they added new equipment, products, and customers, monitoring nonproductive capacity would help them decide how to operate. The team decided to review setups and maintenance before considering the details of waste and standby nonproductive capacity. Suppliers and customers may cause fluctuations in maintenance and the number of setups. However, the IMAC team felt that setup and maintenance were primarily under the control of the internal organization.

EXHIBIT 17

The CAM-1 Capacity Model

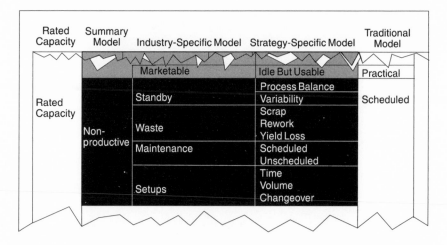

Rated Capacity	Summary Model	Industry-Specific Model	Strategy-Specific Model	Traditional Model
		Marketable	Idle But Usable	Practical
Rated Capacity	Non-productive	Standby	Process Balance Variability	Scheduled
		Waste	Scrap Rework Yield Loss	
		Maintenance	Scheduled Unscheduled	
		Setups	Time Volume Changeover	

 Do not equate nonproductive capacity with "not necessary or not required." Most activities in a process are required until someone changes the process.

Pete noted that the methods the team used to examine nonproductive capacity for a single machine, like the Node-Matic, were applicable to entire production centers. IMAC could make measurements at the machine or facility level. A summary of these measurements as shown in Exhibit 17 would show the total nonproductive capacity. Like Pete, we could use the time and economic data to make a detailed analysis of a process or increments of capacity.

Setups and Maintenance

Setups occur for various reasons. Setups result from changes in the products manufactured or services provided. When a paper mill changes the weight or color of paper, production center use continues but the output is not usable. Other setups occur because of the volume of product produced. For instance, industrial furnaces often require reconditioning after a certain volume of production. Other setups result from the passage of time. We must often clean equipment after particles collect. Whatever the reason for a setup, this use of capacity is nonproductive.

An analysis of setup capacity use provides operating and management teams with opportunities to improve decisions. How much nonproductive capacity relates to setups varies by industry and strategic focus. If a company uses a focused factory, the setups that result from product changeovers are small. However, the company has limited flexibility to meet changing customer needs. Conversely, if a company chooses to manufacture multiple products in the same factory, the amount of setup time is more significant. This might cause setup reduction to become a specific objective for the operating team.

Maintenance is a normal part of operating activities. A company has scheduled and unscheduled maintenance. While we would like all maintenance to be scheduled and preventive, unscheduled maintenance always exists. All maintenance uses capacity because we do not produce good output during maintenance. Highlighting the time and cost of unscheduled maintenance, using the capacity model, helps avoid the temptation to delay regular preventive maintenance when demand for the product or service is high.

During maintenance or setup, a production center does not produce saleable products. While the center is nonproductive, it is not considered idle.

Waste

Waste is another nonproductive use of capacity. In the capacity model, we use a narrow definition of waste and focus on three types of waste: **scrap**, **rework**, and **yield loss**. If we are unable to use a board because we set the machine parameters incorrectly, scrap exists. The scrap uses capacity but does not use it productively. A clear identification of the capacity associated with scrap may allow us to redesign or reengineer the process. These changes may occur internally. Highlighting the cost of this waste may help us work with customers and suppliers to change product or service specifications.

All rework efforts are undesirable. The rework consumes capacity and shows that the process is not producing at 100 percent quality. If IMAC produces a flawed Node-X, it reprocesses the unit. This rework time is not available for producing good units. The existence of idle capacity does not eliminate the need to report rework as a nonproductive use of capacity.

Yield loss also consumes capacity. Yield loss includes anything less than the maximum theoretical conversion of capacity into good products. The IMAC team discussed whether standard yield losses should be part of capacity analysis. Part of the team argued that losses always occur and that separate measures were not worthwhile. Other team members argued that while the company may never achieve a perfect yield, excluding yield loss from the capacity analysis only buries the problem. Exclusions also prevent improvement analysis and make it more difficult to assign responsibility. Therefore, anything short of 100 percent is a nonproductive use of capacity.

> *All scrap, rework, and yield loss is nonproductive. Measures of waste should give visibility to these capacity uses.*

A company may identify waste at the time or place of occurrence. It may also identify waste during any later part of the process. We assign this waste, in "throughput to sales," to each production center or process step that worked on the product. Work done correctly on a product that we cannot sell is not a good use of capacity. If we correctly insert a screw into a flawed product, our insertion effort was not productive. We cannot exchange this product for cash. Measuring this process-level waste helps all work areas maximize global, not local, capacity.

Standby Variability and Process Balance

Standby capacity, not to be confused with idle capacity, exists for two reasons. The first is buffer capacity required to deal with variability, such as the arrival rate of materials or the distribution of capacity down times. The second reason is process balance capacity. This results when areas of the factory can produce at higher output rates than the factory constraint. Application templates, described in Chapter 3, expand on these definitions.

Variability is a primary cause of nonproductive capacity. The IMAC team realized there could be standby capacity in their plant because of short-term variability in customer demands, supplier deliveries, and material flow. These variations result from short run scheduling decisions and the randomness in many processes. This variability is a form of waste. However, the capacity model allows us to separate standby variability from the waste sources discussed above. The reasons standby variability exists are different. The methods an organization uses to reduce this variability are often more complex.

The cumulative total of a company's, plant's, or department's variability and waste is the total waste and variability from suppliers, customers, and internal activities (Exhibit 18).

Suppliers can cause nonproductive capacity by designing materials and parts that do not meet specifications. This makes incoming inspection necessary and increases the potential for scrap or rework. A supplier delivering in quantities that are too large or too small means we have excess inventory management costs or experience process shutdowns. Companies have programs under way to qualify suppliers as strategic suppliers. The requirements include delivery of the right quantity with zero defects and focusing on reducing nonproductive uses of capacity.

EXHIBIT 18

The Cumulative Variability

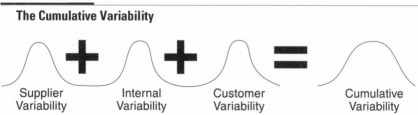

| Supplier Variability | Internal Variability | Customer Variability | Cumulative Variability |

The cumulative variability from several small sources can have a significant impact on capacity use.

> *JIT, KANBAN, and other inventory-led initiatives used inventory reduction to identify the process changes needed to reach the objective of variability and waste reduction. Uninformed process owners sometimes treat these initiatives only as inventory reduction programs. They quickly discover that inventory reduction, after a certain point, without variability and waste reduction, results in lower output.*

Capital equipment suppliers can cause nonproductive capacity by designing equipment with large output volumes, machines that are not flexible, and equipment with reliability problems. If a company must have backup machines available because of frequent failures in the primary production centers, large amounts of nonproductive capacity exist.

People suppliers, our educational institutions, can also cause nonproductive capacity. They may provide a workforce that does not have the necessary analytical and communicative skills to function in the modern technology-driven organization. The inability of people to function in teams may result in significant nonproductive capacity.

While suppliers or customers may be a primary cause of standby variability, internal decisions are a major influence on nonproductive capacity. A human resource department decision to hire the cheapest labor may increase the nonproductive capacity. A decision by engineering to invest in the newest and fastest equipment may result in waste.

Internal variability and waste come from thousands of sources. These range from a common setup, to a power failure caused by an auto wreck in the company parking lot. Internal and external variability requires the manufacturing team to choose between reserving capacity, holding additional inventory, or risking less than scheduled production. This reserve capacity is "buffer capacity." When a company understands its internal variability, it makes better decisions. Reducing the need for a buffer, and then the buffer itself, can result in additional output capability or capital avoidance.

> *The common defense available to manufacturing (or any process owner) is to build inventory or excess capacity as a buffer to guard against variability and waste. Efforts in JIT, KANBAN, and inventory-led initiatives begin exposing causes of variability and waste. The capacity model is another tool companies can use in this area.*

Other nonproductive uses of capacity may exist. For example, adding capacity may require lengthy installation and many qualification runs.

Customer variability and waste can come from many sources. Business cycles, seasonal cycles, erratic order flows, and customers unsure of their needs all influence the amount of standby capacity a company must have available. The revenue generated by providing quick response for customers may be high. However, the standby capacity needed for this quick turn response is nonproductive. The capacity model helps us measure the time and economic effect of a decision to be a "quick turn" supplier. This information can also help us reduce cycle times by producing and then using stored capacity when this is beneficial to the company.

Slowdown can be a disguised form of nonproductive capacity. Equipment age or the inability to execute to the original specification may result in slowdown. Sometimes the slowdown represents a trade-off for improving yields or is a response to a design for manufacturability problem. Slowdowns are part of nonproductive capacity.

> *Rated capacity uses a time measure. It assumes 24 hours a day, 7 days a week, with each tool producing at benchmark rates. The cost of this capacity is the total cost assignable to the process.*

Process balance, also called factory balance or production center balance, exists in most companies. In simple terms, this is the capacity in a nonconstraint production center that is greater than the constraint. Assume that equipment set alpha is the constraint. Set

EXHIBIT 19

Process Balance

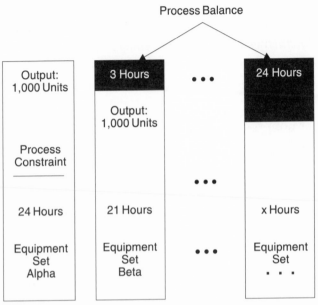

Process balance is capacity that is greater than the process constraint.

alpha can produce only 1,000 units a day. All other equipment sets will average 1,000 units a day in output. If any other equipment sets average more than 1,000 units a day, this only results in increased work in process inventory (Exhibit 19).

If equipment set beta needs only 21 hours of productive and nonproductive time to average 1,000 units a day, then 3 hours is process balance capacity. *Process balance capacity is an opportunity for improvement.* We can improve by working with suppliers, factory to factory capacity management, and by abandonment of unneeded capacity. Process balance is nonproductive capacity in the model.

Process balance capacity is not a source for buffering the constraint. Reserve capacity needed to buffer the constraint due to variability is a form of standby capacity that we label *standby-variability*. Reducing variability or improving productivity in a nonconstraint area results in an increase in what we classify as *standby-process balance* capacity until the company takes additional actions.

Countless examples of nonproductive capacity exist. The capacity model, coupled with a pareto approach and other static and dynamic modeling tools, is a starting point for understanding, defining, measuring, and communicating.

As Pete meets with his IMAC team he says, "For a term defined as 'what is not idle and what is not productive,' it looks like we have a powerful analysis tool. I really want to discuss this with our business teams." Pete also notes that the levels of nonproductive capacity in different industries or plants should be obvious when we examine the model details. The strategic implications are also more visible with this model than with traditional capacity tools.

PRODUCTIVE CAPACITY

Productive capacity provides value to the customer (Exhibit 20). We use productive capacity to change a product or provide a service. Examples of productive use of capacity include these: cutting, molding, welding, painting, furnace time, and assembly. Productive capacity results in the delivery of good products or services. It may also represent the use of capacity for process or product develop-

EXHIBIT 20

Productive Capacity

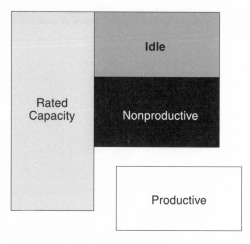

Which capacity is productive?

ment. Productive capacity use is desirable. All companies would like to increase the portion of their capacity that is productive.

Traditional capacity measures are of only limited help in determining when capacity is in a productive state. Terms like "practical capacity" and "standard values for inventory" do not address idle or nonproductive uses of capacity. This is a particular concern when companies engage in quality initiatives or other improvement efforts. Reaching or passing the practical or standard measure presents a picture of great accomplishment. However, nonproductive and wasteful capacity remain hidden in these measures (Exhibit 21).

The model makes clear the difference between productive capacity and practical capacity. An action that is necessary in the current environment does not automatically qualify as productive. The model gives visibility to nonproductive uses of capacity, such as setups, maintenance, training, and wait time. These nonproductive uses are a necessary part of practical capacity, but the model separates productive from nonproductive capacity.

EXHIBIT 21

The CAM-I Capacity Model

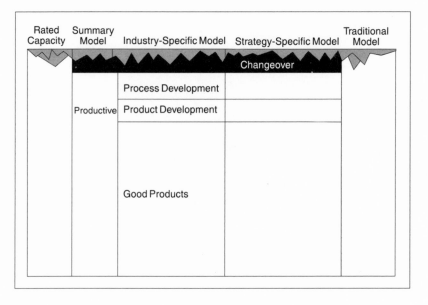

Judy continues to review productive capacity for the IMAC team. She reminds them that the production of good products or the delivery of services is usually to an external customer. However, some customers of the manufacturing process may be other parts of the business. Organizations often use production capacity to develop new processes or new products. These activities add value to the company's future product portfolio. However, these activities, while they consume capacity, do not make product for current sale. The capacity model allows us to segregate these efforts and make their consumption of capacity visible.

Process and Productive Development

Exactly what qualifies as a use of productive capacity, particularly from process and product development, may be difficult to determine. One factor is a company's strategy and industry grouping. If a company's strategy is to execute product and process development in a product lab, using regular production factories for these purposes is not productive. If a company's strategy is to use regular production facilities for product development, this is a productive use of capacity.

A company's state of technology helps us determine productive capacity. In companies that push technology to the limit or where practice is leading recognized theory, conducting a test may be a productive use of capacity. Leading edge semiconductor manufacturing is an example. Tests may also be a productive use of capacity where all products are different, or where the potential liability is so large that testing is a critical part of the production process. Satellite production is an example. However, when well-documented and understood rules of physics and chemistry exist, we can design controls into the process. These controls make tests a nonproductive use of capacity.

 Caution: Never take productive capacity for granted. Advances in the sciences will always alter productive uses of capacity.

Good Products

Good products are the major part of productive capacity in most organizations. For example, IMAC expects to use the Node-Matic machine exclusively for producing Node-X for outside customers. The general rule is this: *The productive use of capacity results in tangible changes in the product or service that are of value to the customer.*

Assume the first work station spends 40 percent of its time in a productive state. Later in the process there is a 50 percent yield loss. Only 20 percent of the work from station 1 reaches the customer. Therefore, only 20 percent of the first work station time and cost qualify as productive capacity. The remaining 20 percent is waste and nonproductive. A phrase that parallels this is "throughput to sales." The capacity model gives us economic information on the effects of improvements in how our company uses productive capacity.

SUMMARY

Pete and the team began to share the model with various IMAC management teams. These teams quickly saw the potential of the model and greeted it with enthusiasm! Product line managers and the research and development groups felt they would be able to see the overall cost of product development. The impact of product design on manufacturability had visibility. The model expanded on, and was a complement to, the company's activity-based product costing effort and management's focus on improvement.

The new capacity model also delighted top management. For the first time they would have capacity information that would give them a strategic global look at capacity. They could see how capital acquisitions fit with existing capacity. They felt this new industry standard would allow better coordination with suppliers and help them consider new outsourcing strategies.

Pete and the team joined the CAM-I effort to continue to refine these basic capacity ideas. In the CAM-I capacity work group Pete learned how other companies were working on the same issues and problems. As the work group examined capacity in service organizations, they found these companies had the same capacity problems and opportunities. The principal difference in the service organizations was that they defined capacity using processes instead of production centers or equipment sets.

Of particular interest was the work that the group was doing to develop specific applications of the capacity model. Pete soon brought IMAC a series of illustrative applications of the capacity model. He also pushed the model as an industry standard that would help IMAC be more effective in communicating to suppliers and customers.

ENDNOTES

1. Ishikawa, Kaoru. *What Is Total Quality Control? The Japanese Way* (Engle-wood Cliffs, NJ: Prentice-Hall, Inc., 1985), p. 45.

2. Vangermersch, Richard. *Alexander Hamilton Church* (New York: Garland Publishing, Inc., 1988), p. 71.

3. Gantt, H. L. *The Relation Between Production and Costs.* Proceedings of the spring meeting of ASME (June 1915), p. 253.

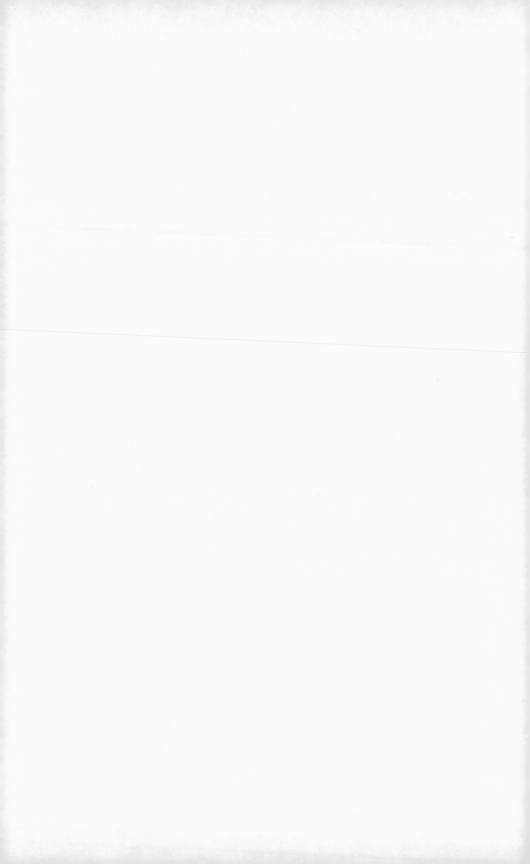

3

CHAPTER

Application Templates

APPLICATIONS—HUB AND SPOKES

The CAM-I Capacity Model is a communication tool a company can apply in many situations. Pete realized the model would provide a fundamental understanding of many capacity issues. Having a common explanation of the several idle, nonproductive, and productive capacity measures is useful.

The key to the capacity model is the focus on both time and economic information. Several applications use this fundamental characteristic of the model. Exhibit 22 depicts common application templates we can extract from the capacity model.

The summary model highlights the total idle, nonproductive, and productive capacity, using color or other coding. This is our fundamental tool for communicating capacity information to upper management. We can use the same template to provide a "quick look" at capacity information for managers at the division or plant level. Knowing the cost of idle time can help managers make better strategic and operating decisions.

Pete knew the team saw the value of capturing and communicating detailed capacity information to the business and operating

EXHIBIT 22

The Many Templates of the CAM-I Capacity Model

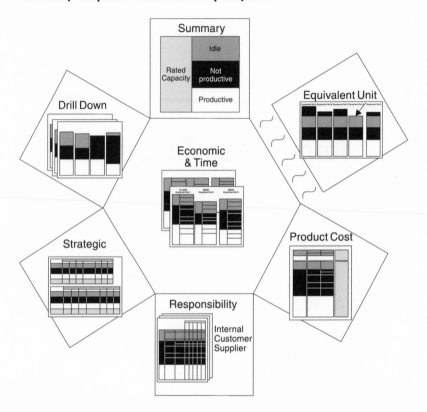

All templates are economic except the equivalent unit template.

teams. This was part of drilling down into the model and adding visibility to the various types of capacity. The combination of the time and economic measurements provided by the model and this drill-down capability gives operations a powerful communication tool.

TIME AND ECONOMIC TEMPLATE

The CAM-I Capacity Model is a collection of capacity data. It includes the supply of capacity. It includes the demand on that capacity by products, maintenance, development, and other uses. Time is

EXHIBIT 23

Time Template

Equipment Set 1		Equipment Set 2		Equipment Set N	
Idle 6 hrs	Not marketable	Idle 7 hrs	Not marketable	Idle 4 hrs	Not marketable
	Off-limits		Off-limits		Off-limits
	Marketable		Marketable		Marketable
Non-productive 10 hrs	Standby	Non-productive 5 hrs	Standby	Non-productive 12 hrs	Standby
	Waste		Waste		Waste
	Maintenance		Maintenance		Maintenance
	Setups		Process Development		Setups
Productive 8 hrs	Process Development	Productive 12 hrs	Product Development	Productive 8 hrs	Process Development
	Product Development				Product Development
	Good Products		Good Products		Good Products

the common element and becomes the raw data used to build the **basic economic template**.

Pete considers this fundamental idea within the context of the capacity that IMAC has in various plants. He reminds the IMAC team that each column represents "all day, every day" for each production center.

> *The time used in each state of capacity varies for each equipment set or production center.*

Pete knows IMAC could prepare a time template such as the one in Exhibit 23 for each of its capacity centers. This time template has considerable value for operations, but is of limited value in providing information to management.

EXHIBIT 24

Basic Economic Template

	$1,000K Equipment Set 1		$800K Equipment Set 2		$900K Equipment Set N
Idle $200K	Not marketable				
	Off-limits			Idle $100K	Not marketable
	Marketable	Idle $200K	Not marketable		Off-limits
	Standby		Off-limits		Marketable
Non-productive $400K	Waste		Marketable	...	Standby
		Non-productive $200K	Standby	Non-productive $500K	Waste
	Maintenance		Waste		
	Setups		Maintenance		Maintenance
Productive $400K	Process Development		Process Development		Setups
	Product Development	Productive $400K	Product Development	Productive $300K	Process Development
	Good Products		Good Products		Product Development
					Good Products

To construct a basic economic template, add process cost to the raw time data and reconstruct the model. This assigns all factory and factory-related costs to the process. These are the equipment sets in this example. The cost includes those for depreciation, leased space, manufacturing labor, engineering support, spares, maintenance contracts, consumables, utilities, and other related items.

> *The implementation section of the primer provides an illustration of how to translate from time to process cost information.*

Unlike the time template, where equal time exists for each capacity set, the basic economic template for each increment of capacity differs (Exhibit 24). The cost of each set is different. Another

EXHIBIT 25

Cost Buildup

characteristic of the template is that the cost for *time* in idle capacity is usually less than an equal amount of *time* in a productive state.

The cost buildup chart in Exhibit 25 is an illustration of this difference. Space and equipment costs usually apply to 24 hours a day. They apply to all three capacity states. Many costs related to people are not present during idle time. People costs exist primarily when we use capacity. However, we must carefully analyze each cost. For example, the costs associated with the people who manage the factory apply to the idle, productive, and nonproductive classifications. We do not pay these individuals more if the factory runs three shifts rather than two.

The costs of consumables—such as gases, electricity to run equipment, and chemicals—accumulate primarily during productive time. We also use these consumables during maintenance, training, and rework. From a process activity costing point of view, and for reporting to management, we separately report a cost for idle, nonproductive, and productive capacity.

This application of fixed and variable costing to activities in a process is not an endorsement for product costing using only variable costs. The product costing application explains which costs should be part of product cost.

DRILL DOWN

The capacity model is built from activities at the operational level and we can report using several different formats. To maximize the strategic value of the model, we need a standard set of substates, performance metrics, and definitions. The CAM-I Capacity Model provides this standard.

Below we describe several economic templates that illustrate the drill-down process. For this illustration, assume we have three

E X H I B I T   26

Company X: Cost of Capacity Summary

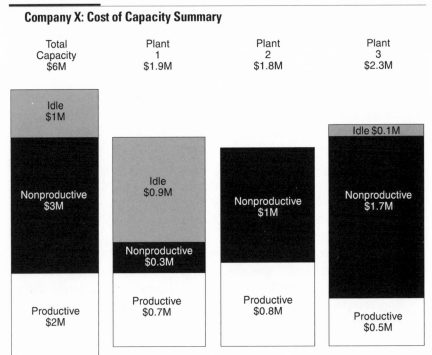

EXHIBIT 27

Company X—Plant 1: Cost of Equipment Capacity

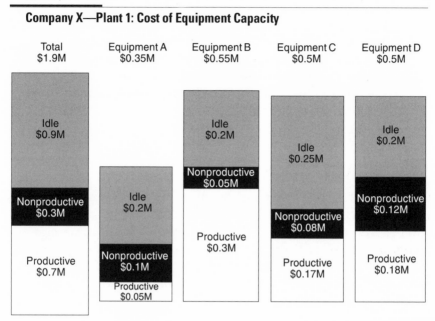

manufacturing plants. Each of these manufacturing plants has four primary equipment sets.

The first template (Exhibit 26) shows an overall capacity report for senior management and shows the dollar cost of these three capacity classes. Differences in each plant are quite visible.

Another template (Exhibit 27) would be for the business team at each plant. The example shows the summary capacities for each piece of equipment in Plant 1. Practically, we would break each capacity category into substates. This would help express to the business team the cost of nonproductive standby, productive development, or idle off-limits, for the plant and on a machine-by-machine basis. The potential levels of detail we can get using drill-down templates should be driven by relevance.

Assume that we had a worldwide group focused on a particular type of equipment. The example (Exhibit 28) shows the summary capacities for equipment B, overall and in each plant. Practically we could break these capacity categories into substates. Our team could show the cost of nonproductive standby or productive development, by plant, or in total for this type of equipment. In effect, we create information to allow us to benchmark ourselves.

 We could provide information in both time and economic terms. However, the basic economic templates are what we would typically use for reporting this information.

STRATEGIC APPLICATION

Peter Drucker[1] states that management's first task is to identify where the organization is today, where it should be, and where it will be. The next step is to decide what actions and resource assignments are necessary to direct the company to where it should be.

The model is a strategic communication tool that is, by design, a communication link from operations to management. We can use it in the annual planning process and the interim update process.

EXHIBIT 28

Company X—Worldwide Equipment Capacity Report: Group B Equipment

Total Equipment B $1.4M	Plant 1 Equipment B $0.55M	Plant 2 Equipment B $0.4M	Plant 3 Equipment B $0.45M
Idle $0.4M	Idle $0.2M	Idle $0.1M	Idle $0.1M
Nonproductive $0.3M	Nonproductive $0.05M	Nonproductive $0.2M	Nonproductive $0.05M
Productive $0.7M	Productive $0.3M	Productive $0.1M	Productive $0.3M

EXHIBIT 29

Capacity Decisions

Strategy —*Drives*→
Product —*Drives*→
Process
Capacity —*Drives*→
Resource
Requirements

Management can use the model to assess the current capacity status, to show trends, and to plan changes in capacity. Manufacturing can use the model to communicate and sell new business initiatives requiring investment and operating changes.

Capacity decisions, along with market segment and product selection, are critical. (See Exhibit 29.) Top management has primary responsibility for the total quantity of capacity, the type of capacity, and the location of capacity. They also decide when to obtain capacity and the segmentation of capacity. For example, they decide whether to produce in one large factory or several small factories.

In acquiring capacity, top management has many strategic concerns. Strategy determines whether we handle external and internal variability with increased inventory, increased capacity, or longer lead times to customers. Other strategic capacity related decisions include these: make versus buy, buy versus lease, buying large chunks of capacity rather than small chunks, and selecting commodity versus custom-designed capacity.

Top management's responsibility for strategic decisions continues after capacity acquisition. For example, how much capacity will a company use for development, a discretionary decision? How should a company allocate capacity to products currently in production? How much diversity should we put in one factory? When should we abandon capacity?

 The CAM-I Capacity Model is primarily a strategic communication tool.

Management must decide how to handle external and internal variability. We can deal with the variability by increasing inventory, increasing capacity, or through longer lead times to customers. For Pete's IMAC factory, the choice was increased capacity. Financial inventory indices are useful in tracking trends and alerting your management to problems. However, we should use them with a good understanding of the trade-offs in dealing with variability. In certain product lines, it may be a wise financial decision to maintain a competitive lead time to customers by increasing inventory. For other products, increasing capacity may be a more profitable option (Exhibit 30).

A company can use capacity in only three ways. It can produce products that it sells to customers today. It can produce products for inventory that we sell to customers tomorrow, or later scrap. Finally, the company might not use the capacity. This is lost capacity that the company can never recover.

> *Capacity can be used in only three ways:*
> *— To produce products for sale today*
> *— To produce products for inventory*
> *— To be lost*

A company may build its basic corporate strategy around a product perspective. Another company may focus on a process perspective. However, whether the product is leading process development or the product is a result of an existing process capability, capacity management remains a key component of the strategy process. Pete asked for clarification of this point. Another capacity team member provided the following examples to help Pete relate these ideas to IMAC.

Many great products were identified long before the processes were built to deliver the products to the market. Examples include Ford's Model T, Dow's magnesium, Jobs's computer, Du Pont's nylon, Carlson's Xerox machine, and Kilby's integrated circuit. Sometimes the product idea led the process by more than 15 years.

A product-led strategy will initially drive the company's level of process capability. After the company establishes the necessary capability, it works process alternatives to improve cost, time, and

EXHIBIT 30

Uses of Capacity

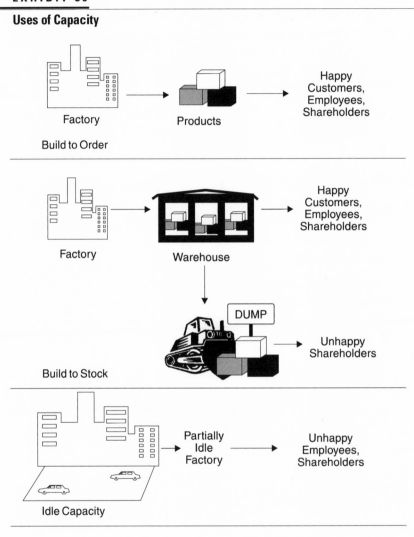

quality. At this point, operations becomes a major factor. Established processes may provide the foundation a company needs to expand into other product markets. Examples include Procter & Gamble's Crisco, Honda's lawnmowers, and McDonald's chicken business.

EXHIBIT 31

Strategic Template: Capacity Use

	Focused vs. Functional				Owned vs. Shared			
	As Is		To Be		As Is		To Be	
	Focused	Functional	Focused	Functional	Owned	Shared	Owned	Shared
Idle	10%				10%			
Nonproductive	30%	20%	25%	20%	40%	15%	35%	10%
Productive	15%	25%	25%	30%	25%	10%	35%	20%
Total	55%	45%	50%	50%	75%	25%	70%	30%

Assume that a company's product strategy calls for high-volume short-cycle time capabilities. A plant with a focused, or product cell, capacity configuration would be consistent with this strategic approach. Plants with a functional capacity configuration would be inconsistent.

Another product strategy may call for a diverse range of low-volume, short-cycle time products. A capacity configuration that invested heavily in flexibility would be consistent with this strategy. Plants that use equipment designed for large batch size would be inconsistent with this strategy.

Capacity model templates help management understand the linkage between capacity and strategy. There are two illustrative templates in Exhibits 31 and 32.

The template in Exhibit 31 allows us to focus on the *use of capacity*. To make strategic decisions, management must understand the capacity that currently exists. It can then plan the type of capacity it wants. Several types of strategic capacity exist. These types include focused capacity, functional capacity, joint venture capacity, balance of trade capacity, and capacity on, or next to, strategic customers' places of business.

Assume that a company's strategy calls for 50 percent of its capacity to be in high-volume commodity products, where cost is the company's competitive advantage. For these products the com-

EXHIBIT 32

Strategic Template: Market Segment

	Last Year			In 3 Years			In 6 Years		
	1	2	>2	1	2	>2	1	2	>2
Idle		5%	10%		10%				
Nonproductive	20%	10%	15%	25%	15%	5%	35%	25%	
Productive	10%	15%	15%	15%	20%	10%	25%	15%	
Total	30%	30%	40%	40%	45%	15%	60%	40%	0%

pany will use functional factories. However, the company will use focused factories to make differentiated products for customers.

The company also prefers to share ownership of the commodity product capacity, but retain full ownership of other capacity. If the company decides to share 60 percent of this commodity capacity, 30 percent of the total capacity requires joint funding.

The template in Exhibit 32 focuses management's attention on the market. A company could show the market by customer. Examples of customer classifications might include strategic, major, minor, international, and government. This would allow management to know what portion of existing idle, productive, and nonproductive capacity exists in each area. They could set targets for future periods.

Another market orientation template might focus on a company's capacity in segments stratified by market dominance. Assume that a strategic objective of our company is to be first or second in each market segment in six years. We could list the capacity according to the products that were first, second, or in another market position.

Each of these strategic templates is built from equipment level and product level activity information. This makes drilling down to sublevels of information possible. This information allows management to see products that are not meeting—and, more important, those products that are exceeding—the plan.

Pete notes in the next IMAC presentation that these templates represent only a few of the strategic applications of the capacity model.

RESPONSIBILITY REPORTING

Questions about capacity and its efficient use are not new. During a raging debate in the early 1900s, H. L. Gantt,[2] wrote a position paper of profound candor and relevance. Gantt asserted that the place to start to improve productivity is to analyze capacity when it is not productive. This analysis included logical groupings of nonproductive activities and the likely department in the organization with the most opportunity for potential improvement.

How much idle, nonproductive, and productive capacity exist? Who is responsible for this capacity and its cost? The capacity model helps us answer these critical questions, particularly when joint responsibility exists. This potential for confusion started IMAC on its capacity journey. Pete was now even more aware that in assigning internal responsibility, IMAC had to consider the effects of their suppliers and customers.

Internal Responsibility

Three groups have primary responsibility for uses of capacity: the business team, the manufacturing team, and the support or enabling teams (see Exhibit 33). The responsibilities of these teams overlap, which makes identification and assignment of responsibility difficult. The model groups activities, thus helping us clarify and communicate responsibility.

The composition of a business team might vary by industry or strategy. At IMAC the business team includes the managers from R&D, engineering, manufacturing, and marketing. The team also includes the business leader. Primary responsibility for the amount of installed capacity, the type or capability of capacity, and the business processes used to manage capacity rests with the business team. This team executes the strategic plan and controls several basic business processes. These processes include product development, planning, and customer communication, including ordering. The team considers how much capacity the business needs in five years. It considers the

EXHIBIT 33

Areas of Joint Responsibility

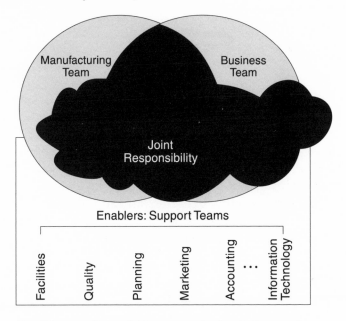

Use the capacity model to remove the fog that prevents effective management of areas of joint responsibility.

type of capacity. In simple terms, the business team is responsible for reducing idle capacity and increasing productive capacity.

Manufacturing teams (or service teams) vary by company, but their primary focus is on operations. At Pete's Node-Matic plant, the team includes manufacturing, equipment engineering, and process engineering. This team has primary responsibility for daily operations, internal variability, work in process inventory, training, quality, equipment variability, and statistical process control. The manufacturing team is responsible for the effective and efficient use of today's capacity. Their primary target is an increase in factory throughput.

An important responsibility of the production, or manufacturing, team is to communicate to the business team. The business team must understand the potential impacts of what they decide before

EXHIBIT 34

Team Responsibilities

Manufacturing Team

Productive

Nonproductive

Idle

Business Team

finalizing their conclusions and spending money. For example, what is the impact of buying two small machines instead of one large machine? What if we add another product line by expanding the existing factory instead of building a focused factory? The production team has a responsibility to understand and communicate these trade-offs to the business team. The model is useful in meeting this communication responsibility (see Exhibit 34).

The manufacturing teams are responsible for reducing nonproductive activities, black, and increasing idle capacity, gray. The business team is responsible for reducing idle capacity and increasing productive capacity, white.

Enabling teams include various support functions. Examples of enabling teams include human resources, finance and accounting, quality, planning, and management information systems. In many companies, these groups are also part of the business and operating teams. The teams represent the infrastructure that exists to support, or enable, the selling and creating side of the business. However a company structures and uses these enabling teams, they influence capacity and capacity management. The processes, policies, and resource development programs of these teams have capacity implications. For responsibility reporting, it is useful to separate enabling teams from the business and operating teams.

One example of how enabling teams influence capacity is found in operator selection, training, and compensation. Trade-offs exist between the cost in these categories and reducing the nonproductive

EXHIBIT 35

Capital Acquisitions

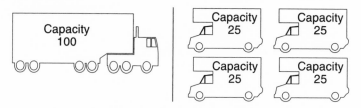

Four smaller-capacity trucks may have more flexibility and less
nonproductive cost, even though the acquisition cost is higher.

use of capacity. Fast-food restaurants design processes for high
productive output using part-time workers while minimizing entry-
level selection, training, and compensation costs. A more technical
process, such as wafer fabrication, uses full-time workers, provides
more training, and pays higher wages to avoid having large amounts
of nonproductive capacity use.

Employee measurement and incentive programs and policies
also positively drive behavior and dramatically affect capacity productivity. Some companies have dedicated maintenance resources
for machines, or even entire processes. The maintenance person is
responsible for the process 24 hours a day. This person has a strong
incentive to make certain that the process continues to function. This
allows him or her to avoid having to commute to the facility and
repair the problem during sleeping hours.

 *The measurement and communication of the states of
capacity are important to the entire enterprise.*

The finance and accounting support team directly influences
manufacturing capacity in many ways. One major effect is in the
capital justification policies many companies use. Assume that a
company has a short payback period requirement for justifying
capital acquisitions. This may cause the company to limp along
with old equipment. Such equipment may require frequent repair,

provide poor quality or yield output, and have a long cycle time. Companies often live with this poor performance because their capital policies require one- to two-year payback periods. This does not allow the companies to match the economic benefit of the capacity investments over realistic time horizons. These short payback practices add to the black, nonproductive capacity, reported in the model.

A company may approve capital acquisitions based on a lowest cost per unit calculation. This causes the company to buy increments of capacity that are larger than necessary. In other companies, the capital procurement process is driven by the lowest price tag, rather than the lowest total cost of ownership. Each of these capital authorization practices can lead a company to acquire nonstandard equipment sets. These may, in turn, limit flexibility, require a resource-intensive support organization, and be misaligned with the strategic direction of manufacturing.

 Another CAM-I monograph, Managing Strategic and Capital Investment Decisions, ***addresses capital investment issues in detail.***

The business processes owned by the enabling teams need to be lean in design. The process must be efficient in output and robust in results to support the business and manufacturing teams. Measuring and communicating the status of capacity helps an organization in its quest to become lean.

Pete decided to work with an IMAC plant and create a responsibility template (see Exhibit 36). The template makes the relative responsibility for each of the industry and strategic capacity groups visible. The template shows the percentage of cost responsibility for each team. If the total cost of scrap was $2 million, the template would show that the manufacturing team was responsible for 60 percent, or $1.2 million, of this cost. The business team, human resources, finance, and other teams each have responsibility for 10 percent, or $200,000, of the scrap capacity cost.

EXHIBIT 36

Responsibility Template (Hypothetical Cost Percentage Responsibility)

			Responsibility				
			Business Team	Manufacturing Team	Suuport Team Human Resources	Support Team Finance	Others
Idle	Not marketable	Excess Not Usable	70%			30%	
	Off-limits	Management Policy	80%			20%	
		Contractual	100%				
		Legal	80%		20%		
	Marketable	Idle But Usable	80%		10%	10%	
Non-productive	Standby	Process Balance	10%	30%	10%	40%	10%
		Variability	20%	30%	10%		40%
	Waste	Scrap	10%	60%	10%	10%	10%
		Rework	10%	60%	10%	10%	10%
		Yield Loss		40%	20%	20%	20%
	Maintenance	Scheduled		80%		20%	
		Unscheduled		60%	20%	10%	10%
	Setups	Time		40%	20%	10%	30%
		Volume		60%		10%	30%
		Changeover	50%		20%	30%	
Productive	Process Development			70%	20%	10%	
	Product Development			80%		20%	
	Good Products				100%		

Customer Responsibility

We can use a similar responsibility template to show the capacity use associated with individual customers, or classes of customers. Pete recalled a discussion about the need for nonproductive standby capacity because of customer variability. An illustrative customer responsibility template for one of IMAC's plants is shown in Exhibit 37. If process balance costs were $1 million, the template shows that Customer A bears responsibility for $200,000 of this cost.

The effect suppliers have on capacity could be summarized in a similar template.

PRODUCT COSTING

Capacity reporting templates that make visible the costs of various types of capacity have implications for product costing (see Exhibit 38). These templates encourage us to examine product costing questions differently. We start with the question, *What types or uses of capacity would exist if the plant was producing at maximum output?* The answer helps us determine what cost to assign to unit production and to inventoriable cost, and what cost is a business or period cost.

This section describes a series of changes in idle capacity reporting. It offers suggestions for changes in internal and external reporting. The steps are shown in Exhibit 38.

Traditional Product Costing

Product costing is a major concern in most organizations. Their current accounting systems often do not provide relevant product costs. If we do not know the cost of providing a product or service, it is difficult to decide which products or services to emphasize. The need for better product cost information is a factor driving the growth of activity accounting. It is also a factor in the growing emphasis on target costing.

Capacity decisions have implications for product costing. Of particular concern in the product costing area is idle capacity. The business team, not the operating team, has primary responsibility for gray, or idle, capacity. However, most manufacturing companies bury the cost of idle capacity in the overhead account. The products

EXHIBIT 37

Customer Responsibility Template (Hypothetical Cost Percentage Responsibility)

			Customer				
			A	B	C	D	Others
Idle	Not marketable	Excess Not Usable					
	Off-limits	Management Policy Contractual Legal					
	Marketable	Idle But Usable	20%	5%	15%		60%
Non-productive	Standby	Process Balance	20%	10%	30%	5%	35%
		Variability	10%		20%	10%	60%
	Waste	Scrap	5%	20%	10%	10%	55%
		Rework		10%	40%	5%	45%
		Yield Loss	25%	30%	15%	15%	15%
	Maintenance	Scheduled					
		Unscheduled					
	Setups	Time	10%	20%	5%	10%	55%
		Volume	30%	20%	15%	5%	30%
		Changeover	20%	15%	50%	5%	10%
Productive	Process Development			20%		10%	70%
	Product Development			5%		20%	75%
	Good Products		30%	20%	15%	5%	30%

produced in the plant bear the cost of the idleness, along with all other costs of operating the business. This occurs because companies use a "rate per unit" calculation for cost assignment.

EXHIBIT 38

Reporting Improvements

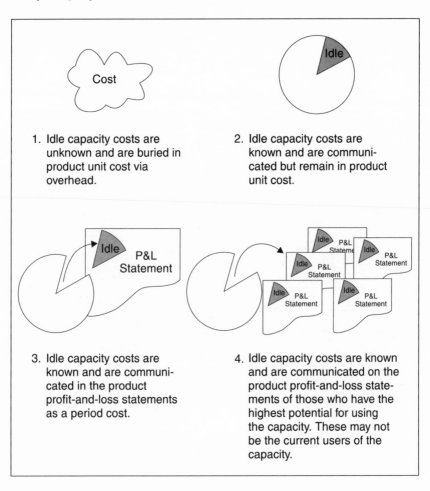

1. Idle capacity costs are unknown and are buried in product unit cost via overhead.

2. Idle capacity costs are known and are communicated but remain in product unit cost.

3. Idle capacity costs are known and are communicated in the product profit-and-loss statements as a period cost.

4. Idle capacity costs are known and are communicated on the product profit-and-loss statements of those who have the highest potential for using the capacity. These may not be the current users of the capacity.

Under traditional "full absorption" accounting, we divide the spending by the volume. We then apply this rate to a product, or to groups of products. This computation accounts for all input costs by applying them to the product for a given period. The costs applied to products the company does not sell in the current period become part of inventory. This is the acceptable way to match revenues and expenses for external financial reporting.

EXHIBIT 39

Charging Idle Capacity to Profit and Loss

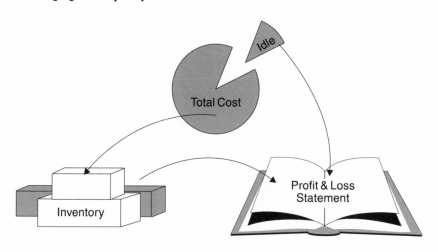

Companies may charge categories of idle capacity cost identified by the model directly to profit and loss (see Exhibit 39). This allows the company to avoid an overstatement of inventory value.

A Different Costing Approach

The capacity model supports the view that idle capacity is a *period cost*. A period cost is attributable to the ongoing cost of running the business. But it is not a cost of the products made, or services performed, during that time. Accountants classify development, marketing, and administrative costs as period expense. Idle capacity costs, such as IMAC's from the large machine purchase, are similar and are logically period costs. These costs relate to the continuing cost of running the business, not to the products made in the plant during this period.

A period cost approach has several advantages. There is a decrease in unit cost. The cost is now representative of the portion of the capacity used in the production process. Plant managers have, in the past, been *de facto* responsible for all the idle capacity. As shown in the example in Table 1, the plant manager is now responsible for only 90 percent of the costs.

TABLE 1

A Period Cost Approach

	Traditional	Proposed
Total Costs	100	100
Idle Capacity Cost	—	10
Product Costs	100	90
Volumes	100	100
Unit Cost	1.00	0.90

TABLE 2

Summary Product Cost Template

Idle (marketable)	10	Cost of Business
Nonproductive	40	Cost of Production
Productive	50	

> *Not all idle capacity is chargeable to period cost; it depends on the root cause of the idle capacity. (See the detailed product cost template in Exhibit 40.)*

We can also make each type of capacity more visible. Knowing that 10 percent of the product cost is due to idle capacity allows management to focus on using or eliminating this capacity. Often idle capacity exists because management believes demand will increase. This is idle, but useable, capacity. Sometimes anticipated demand never materializes. Then the capacity is excess and not useable. While manufacturing plays a role in such a failed prediction, marketing and other organizational units also have an impact on predicting market volumes.

Table 2 shows a simple example of the product costing template that comes from the capacity model. Assume that a factory with 10 percent idle capacity also has 40 percent nonproductive capacity. Setups, maintenance, waste, and variability are components of this nonproductive capacity. The factory needs this capacity to build a product in the current environment. This nonproductive, or black (red) capacity is a cost of production, not a cost of business.

The capacity model allows us to refine the product costing template. Idle capacity that is marketable and not marketable represents a cost of business. However, idle capacity that is off-limits is part of the product cost. Whether the capacity is off-limits because of legal restrictions, contractual obligations, or management policy, these costs are a necessary part of product cost in the current environment.

The product costing template assigns nonproductive uses of capacity to period costs. Exceptions to this classification may exist when there are unusual nonproductive uses of capacity. For example, if a company has a major flood, a chemical spill, or other major disruption that shuts down a factory for several days, these costs are logically part of period costs.

If we use the capacity model for product costing, the cost of developing future products and future capabilities is not part of the cost of current unit production. An illustration of the restructured capacity model, separating the cost of business from the product cost is found in Exhibit 40.

> *The suggestions made in the product costing section are consistent with generally accepted accounting principles.*

Focusing on factory capacity and the associated cost should strengthen traditional cost accounting methods. Separating idle capacity costs and accounting for these costs logically give needed relief to operations. For too long, unit costs have borne the full cost of idle capacity. This has made the plant manager solely responsible for conditions that he or she alone did not create.

Idle capacity has a cost. We should make this cost explicit. This idle marketable and nonmarketable cost should be a period charge and not applied to products. This is important information for business management that the financial community can provide.

EXHIBIT 40

Detailed Product Cost Template

Idle	Not marketable	Excess Not Usable	Cost
	Marketable	Idle But Usable	of
Productive	Process Development Product Development		Business

Idle	Off-limits	Management Policy Contractual Legal	
Non-productive	Standby	Process Balance	Product
		Variability	Cost
	Waste	Scrap Rework Yield Loss	
	Maintenance	Scheduled	
		Unscheduled	
	Setups	Time Volume Changeover	
Productive	Good Products		

CONSTRAINT OR EQUIVALENT UNITS TEMPLATE

The focus of the capacity model is the entire process. The constraint or equivalent units template allows us to focus attention on the process, the capacity, that limits the production of good products. This is the constraint.

The template allows us to communicate the level of process balance that exists in equipment sets that do not constrain capacity. These are nonconstraints. This template makes the constraint and nonconstraint equipment sets visible. This template is not a time or economic template, it is an equivalent units template that focuses on the level of process balance.

The CAM-I Capacity Model is a process measure, not a traditional equipment capacity measure. The model makes three capacity substates visible: standby—process balance, waste—downstream, and idle marketable. The process constraint defines how much capacity is idle marketable.

We may be able to identify the constraint by walking around the plant. In other situations, the constraint is difficult to recognize. If a company continually introduces products, new processes, additional equipment, and mix changes, the constraint constantly changes. However, even in complex environments, constraint management should receive a high priority. The capacity model is a tool that helps us communicate improvement opportunities.

The constraint in the process defines the throughput of the entire process. In simple terms, if the constraint can process only 1,000 units that can be sold to customers, all other equipment sets will process 1,000 units. Although the other equipment sets could produce more, the constraint paces all processes. Given this manufacturing rule, we may also call the constraint template an equivalent unit's template.

In the template in Exhibit 41, equipment set D is the constraint. All other equipment sets will have nonproductive standby capacity, process balance, because of this constraint.

Often management intentionally provides process balance capacity in nonconstraint equipment sets. This is a way of protecting the constraint in the existing environment. This may raise the question, Why is the process balance black capacity? Process balance is black, or nonproductive, capacity because, although it exists in today's environment, the capacity model suggests that we should get rid of the need for this capacity. This is similar to saying that planned maintenance has value. The model still identifies this as nonproductive capacity, because we want to eliminate the need even for planned maintenance. We want an engine to run forever without a tuneup.

EXHIBIT 41

Constraint or Equivalent Units Template for Equipment Sets A–D and N

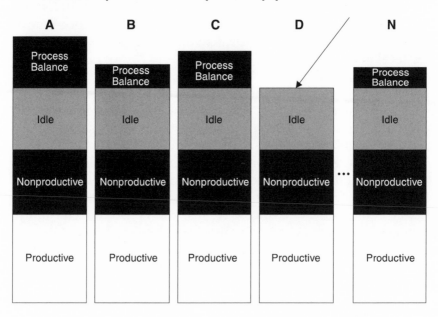

 During short periods, nonconstraint equipment may produce at higher or lower throughput rates. However, with good inventory management practices in place, these are minimal. From a strategic view, these fluctuations in work in process do not warrant special reporting.

SUMMARY

There are many other application templates that we might derive from the CAM-I Capacity Model. What the illustrative templates and the explanations show are the potential the model provides for more effectively managing capacity.

Pete and his IMAC team realize that the most difficult phase of the journey is the implementation. The actual process of measuring the economic cost of various states of capacity will require a management belief that the results will support better business decisions.

ENDNOTES

1. Drucker, Peter F. *Management Tasks, Responsibilities, Practices* (New York: Harper & Row, 1974), p. 122.
2. Miller, F. G., et al. *Biography of Henry Laurence Gantt*, "H. L. Gantt's Contribution to Industry." ASME Transactions, Vol. 42 (1920), p. 417.

4

CHAPTER

Implementation Examples

The capacity model provides a flexible approach to understanding and managing capacity processes. The model is useful for firms that provide services, provide goods, do assembly, and do high-value-added manufacturing. The model also applies to government organizations. We can use the model to focus attention on types of capacity information and report capacity costs in many ways. We can tailor each report to specific objectives.

Implementation is an important part of the CAM-I Capacity Model adoption. A detailed examination of implementation issues is beyond the scope of this primer. However, there are three examples of implementation processes. The first is a brief discussion of the use of ABC costing to help measure capacity cost. The second and third illustrate how we could communicate the economic cost of capacity in a service function and in a production function.

> *One important implementation note: The model is not a management exercise where we "buy software and plug it in." We will use software to construct the model, but this is the last item to consider.*

Finally, the following section provides a summary of common implementation steps.

COSTING METHODOLOGY FOR ECONOMIC TRANSLATION

The model is an economic mirror of operations, the process. With this economic conversion, management is less likely to receive misleading information.

To illustrate, Pete describes an example from an IMAC plant. "The plant has a 10-year-old furnace operation that requires little space, minimal maintenance, and only a part-time operator. Plant operators use this incremental capacity for productive activities 10 percent of the time. The asset is nonproductive 90 percent of the time. This low usage is driven by two criteria. The first is the low time requirement of each product. The second is the upstream constraint in the factory. The constraint is a multimillion-dollar, high-precision, flexible machine tool. We use this machine tool for productive activities 40 percent of the time and for nonproductive activities 60 percent of the time. Without an economic conversion from time to dollars, the model would call management's attention to the furnace, rather than the flexible machining tool."

Identifying cost is one task of capacity and process management. How do we get the capacity costs? The recommended costing methodology is to use activities. If you are familiar with activity-based costing (ABC), the model is in the center box in the ABC diagram (see Exhibit 42). Using the model in the understanding and the management of process is the horizontal section of the ABC diagram.

For those who are not familiar with ABC, in simple terms, we use the following steps to obtain a cost measure:

1. Identify an area of the organization with known boundaries. These boundaries include a manufacturing facility, a focused factory, or another known process. For the following steps, assume a manufacturing facility.

2. Identify logical subunits of the factory, such as receiving, cutting, grinding, assembly, painting, finishing, inspection, packing, shipping, planning, and administration.

EXHIBIT 42

An Activity-Based Costing Model

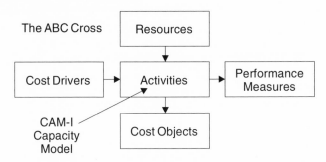

3. Identify resource units, usually cost centers, that wholly or partially support the factory.

4. Identify logical resource pools contained in the cost centers, such as people, equipment, spares, space, consumables, and utilities.

5. Identify resource drivers that map the resource pools to the subunits and activities within the subunits. Resource drivers include these: head count assignment or hours for people, direct assignment for equipment and spares, floor space for space, direct or allocated assignment for consumables and utilities.

6. Compute the cost per resource driver. Examples include these: depreciation and lease dollars per head count, per square foot, and per equipment.

7. Map the resource cost from the cost centers to the subunits of capacity via the resource drivers.

Apply pareto guidelines when completing steps two through five.

 For additional reading on ABC, refer to An ABC Manager's Primer *published by CAM-I and the Institute of Management Accountants.*

SERVICE APPLICATION

Capacity is a process issue. In simple terms, a process is a set of activities that includes inputs, conversion, and outputs. Communication of the capacity is the aim of the capacity model. Processes and process management are as relevant to a service or service industry as they are to manufacturing. The following service example illustrates how we might apply the model.

Case Facts

Assume we have an accounts payable department that provides bill-paying services to several major corporations. The department works two shifts, five days per week. The department has capacity people to process 40,000 payments (checks) per week.

A time analysis of the activities that are part of the overall process shows the following:

- The department spends 45 percent of the time issuing 30,000 checks. This is productive time.
- Opening mail takes 5 percent of the time. This is analogous to a setup in a manufacturing environment.
- Resolving problems with suppliers takes 30 percent of the time.
- Errors that require the staff to rework 6,000 checks take 20 percent of the time.

The last three activities are nonproductive. While they are necessary, they do not add to the department's output.

The total budget for the department is $372,000. The budget detail is as follows:

- $100,000 for continually available space and computers (24 hours).
- $200,000 for people for two shifts.
- $72,000 for consumables ($2 per check for paper costs).

Data for Time and Quantity Template

The processing personnel have the ability to produce 40,000 checks a week. Actual good checks produced are 30,000 and there are 6,000 checks reworked.

Available output capacity—40,000	100%
Less actual output—30,000 + 6,000	90%
Idle capacity—lack of demand	10%

We then analyze how the department uses the 90 percent active time.

Opening mail (5% × 90%)	4%
Supplier problems (30% × 90%)	27%
Rework (20% × 90%)	18%
Process good checks (45% × 90%)	41%
Active time	90%

We do a similar analysis to compute the portion of available equipment time spent in various capacity states. The equipment is available 24 hours a day, but used when there are processing clerks.

Available time (7 days × 24 hours = 168 hours)	100%
Equipment use (5 days × 16 hours = 80 hours)	48%
Idle time (88 hours)	52%

We analyze the department use of the equipment during the 48 percent scheduled time. While the equipment was in use, it could process 40,000 checks but actually processed only 36,000 checks, or 90 percent of the capacity.

Process capacity while equipment available (40,000)	48%
Checks processed (36,000) (90% x 48%)	43%
Idle, no demand (10% × 48%)	5%

Next we analyze how the department uses the equipment during the 43 percent of the time it was in active use.

Opening mail (5% × 43%)	2%
Supplier problems (30% x 43%)	13%
Rework (20% × 43%)	9%
Process good checks (45% × 43%)	19%
Active time	43%

We now have the data we need to prepare the time and quantity template (Exhibit 43).

EXHIBIT 43

Time and Quantity Template—Accounts Payable Example

	Equip/Space	People	Consumables
Idle—Off-limits	52%		
Idle—Market Demand	5%	10%	
Nonproductive—Setups	2%	4%	
Nonproductive—Supplier	13%	27%	
Nonproductive—Rework	9%	18%	6,000
Productive	19%	41%	30,000
Total	100%	100%	36,000

Economic Template

In this example the budget numbers provide the information needed to convert the time template to an economic template. Here are examples of what the economic template shows.

Since management determined that the accounts payable department would work only two shifts five days a week, 52 percent or $52,000 of the equipment cost was idle—off-limits. The processing staff spent 27 percent of their time resolving supplier problems. This means we assign $54,000 of the $200,000 people cost as nonproductive—supplier. Since each check, good or rework, costs $2, the productive cost of consumables was $60,000. An accounts payable example is shown as Exhibit 44. In Exhibit 45, a familiar pareto analysis visually shows this capacity analysis.

PRODUCTION APPLICATION

The following manufacturing example illustrates how we might apply the model to communicate process management capacity information. The example parallels the service model illustrated in the prior section.

EXHIBIT 44

Economic Template—Accounts Payable Example

	Equip/Space	People	Consumables	Total
Idle—Off-limits	A $52,000			$52,000
Idle—Market Demand	$5,000	$20,000		$25,000
Nonproductive—Setups	$2,000	$8,000		$10,000
Nonproductive—Supplier	$13,000	B $54,000		$67,000
Nonproductive—Rework	$9,000	$36,000	$12,000	$57,000
Productive	$19,000	$82,000	C $60,000	$161,000
Total	$100,000	$200,000	$72,000	$372,000

A. 52% x $100,000 (Total cost of space and computers)
B. 27% x $200,000 (total cost of people)
C. 30,000 x $2 (Cost of each check)

EXHIBIT 45

Economic Pareto Analysis—Accounts Payable Example

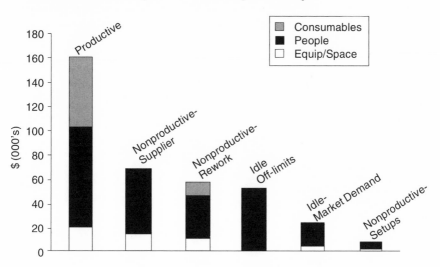

Case Facts

Assume we have a packaging department that services the manufacturing line of the firm. The department works two shifts, five days per week. The department has the capacity to package 60,000 products per week.

A time analysis of the activities that are part of the overall process shows the following:

- The department spends 45 percent of the time packaging 45,000 items. This is productive time.
- Preparing for different products takes 30 percent of the time. This is a form of setup.
- Resolving problems with packaging suppliers takes 5 percent of the time.
- Errors that require the associates to repackage 9,000 products take 20 percent of the time.

The last three activities are nonproductive. While they are necessary, they do not add to the department's output.

The total budget for the department is $558,000. The budget detail is as follows:

- $150,000 for continually available space and packaging machines (24 hours)
- $300,000 for people for two shifts
- $108,000 for consumables ($2 per package for materials)

Data for Time and Quantity Template

The packaging personnel have the ability to package 60,000 products a week. Actual good packages produced are 45,000 and there are 9,000 packages reworked.

Available output capacity—60,000	100%
Less actual output—45,000 + 9,000	90%
Idle capacity—lack of demand	10%

We then analyze how the department uses the 90 percent active time.

Line preparation (30% × 90%)	27%
Supplier problems (5% × 90%)	4%
Rework (20% × 90%)	18%
Good packaging (45% × 90%)	41%
Active time	90%

We do a similar analysis to compute the portion of available equipment time spent in various capacity states. The equipment is available 24 hours a day, but used when there are packing associates working.

Available time (7 days × 24 hours = 168 hours)	100%
Equipment use (5 days × 16 hours = 80 hours)	48%
Idle time (88 hours)	52%

We analyze the department use of the equipment during the 48 percent scheduled time. While the equipment is in use, it can process 60,000 packages but actually processes only 54,000 packages, or 90 percent of the capacity.

Process capacity while equipment available (60,000)	48%
Packages processed (54,000) (90% × 48%)	43%
Idle, no demand (10% × 48%)	5%

Next we analyze how the department uses the equipment during the 43 percent of the time it is in active use.

Setting equipment (30% × 43%)	13%
Supplier problems (5% × 43%)	2%
Rework (20% × 43%)	9%
Process good packages (45% × 43%)	19%
Active time	43%

We now have the data we need to prepare the time and quantity template (Exhibit 46).

EXHIBIT 46

Time and Quantity Template—Packaging Example

	Equip/Space	People	Consumables
Idle—Off-limits Idle—Market Demand	52% 5%	10%	
Nonproductive—Setups Nonproductive—Supplier	13% 2%	27% 4%	
Nonproductive—Rework	9%	18%	9,000
Productive	19%	41%	45,000
Total	100%	100%	54,000

Economic Template

In this extension of the packaging example the budget numbers provide the information needed to convert the time template to an economic template. Here are examples of what the economic template shows.

Since management determined that the packaging department would work only two shifts five days a week, 52 percent or $78,000 of the equipment cost was idle—off-limits. The processing clerks spent 27 percent of their time dealing with line preparation. This means $81,000 of the $300,000 people cost is assigned to nonproductive—setups. Since each package, good or rework, costs $2, the productive cost of consumables was $90,000. Exhibit 47 provides an economic template for packaging, and Exhibit 48 shows a pareto analysis of this data.

EXHIBIT 47

Economic Template—Packaging Example

	Equip/Space	People	Consumables	Total
Idle—Off-limits	A $78,000			$78,000
Idle—Market Demand	$7,500	$30,000		$37,500
Nonproductive—Setups	$19,500	B $81,000		$100,500
Nonproductive—Supplier	$3,000	$12,000		$15,000
Nonproductive—Rework	$13,500	$54,000	$18,000	$85,500
Productive	$28,500	$123,000	C $90,000	$241,500
Total	$150,000	$300,000	$108,000	$558,000

A. 52% x $150,000 (Total cost of space and equipment)
B. 27% x $300,000 (Total cost of people)
C. 45,000 x $2 (Cost of each package)

EXHIBIT 48

Economic Pareto Analysis—Packaging Example

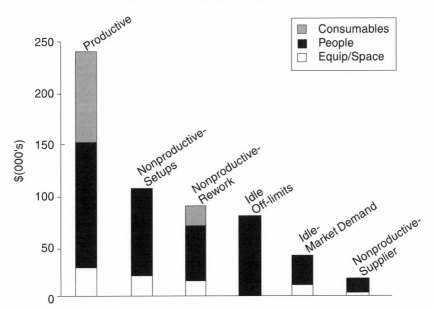

5 CHAPTER

Implementation Procedures

How a company implements the capacity model depends on the company's focus and the driving organizational unit. Initial model development should use historical data from the targeted area of capacity management. This focus helps develop an understanding of the current capacity process environment.

Applying the model to projections will provide the most value. In the future application mode, the model will provide input to product investment decisions, capacity authorization decisions, strategic supplier management decisions, and strategic customer management decisions.

Listed below is a series of steps that are helpful in implementing the capacity model. Following the list is a brief discussion of each step.

1. Organize the implementation team.
2. Determine management objectives.
3. Select a model presentation template.
4. Review element definitions.
5. Select the measurement period.

6. Identify and access operational data.

7. Identify and access financial data.

8. Summarize to level of required presentation model.

9. Monitor for results.

1. Organize the implementation team

Successful implementation of the capacity model requires senior management and operating teams to reach a consensus on the need for the model information. Without a consensus, the implementation has little chance for success.

Many organizations choose to use a teaming environment when implementing factorywide and companywide procedures or applications. This requires the involvement of personnel from the business, manufacturing (operating), and enabling teams. This cross-functional team receives education and training. They then build consensus and take responsibility for the education and training of others in the organization.

2. Determine management objectives

The model is a communication tool for influencing the investment decision processes. This requires the identification and communication of management objectives. Without these objectives, we cannot use the model effectively.

The objectives may include these: strategic supplier management practices, idle capacity resolution (downsizing), increasing capacity flexibility, and identifying causes of variability and waste in the factory. The company may also be trying to move from a functional to a focused factory layout.

Each of these objectives influences the activities identified by the model and the presentation template(s).

3. Select a model presentation template

Different capacity templates support different business objectives. Assume a company has a high percentage of idle capacity. An idle capacity template can communicate the different types of idle capacity. It can provide economic information on the market segment and regional location of the idle capacity.

If the market demand exceeds capacity supply, then a capacity template could focus on nonproductive capacity. This would help us show the various types and sources of variability and waste.

The application section of the primer illustrates several different presentation templates a company might use.

4. Review element definitions

When implementing something new it is tempting to create a new glossary of terms specific to the undertaking. The capacity model is not a new management procedure. It is a communication tool. It uses the language and definitions already in use in the organization. However, if we apply the model to multiple factories and a common language does not exist between these factories, we need to establish a set of common terms. Without a common language, it is difficult, and perhaps impossible, to be effective in implementing the model.

In some industries, established industry standards of communication exist. For example, in the semiconductor industry, the SEMI E10 is the standard state of capacity language.

5. Select the measurement period

The model focuses on strategic decision processes. Measures that use quarterly and annual periods are typically more useful than daily and weekly reporting periods. In fact, frequent updates may contain distortions that would be harmful if used to make strategic decisions. More frequent measures may have value at certain operating levels.

6. Identify and access operational data

The model is an economic mirror of existing capacity. We use states of capacity that are already defined to operations and used in the management process. The model, by design, identifies activities that influence decisions. If the identified activities are not a part of current operations management, giving attention to the activities will probably not result in action.

7. Identify and access financial data

The model allows us to focuses on a subprocess within a larger process or activities within a process. Companies with ABC systems probably already have financial data for these processes and activities. For companies using traditional overhead cost assignments, opportunities for improvement exist. The capacity model can help a company assign overhead to the most appropriate process and activity.

For product costing purposes there may be costs, such as labor or consumables, that can be directly traced and assigned to a product. ABC suggests assigning these costs to a process to ensure adequate visibility when making process improvement decisions. For example, package material may be identified directly to products. Different grades of package material may have a major impact on setup times, types of equipment, and process variability. For ABC and capacity model reporting, this package cost is part of the packaging process.

8. Summarize to level of required presentation model

The team responsible for machine capacity management will require more detailed information than the manufacturing team. The manufacturing team will require more detailed information than the business management team. Summary data is important to ensure that each level can understand capacity effects on their areas of responsibility.

9. Monitor for results

Activities in the factory are many. As a result, we apply the pareto principle to the capacity model to ensure that the users focus on the two or three most important areas of opportunity. Monitoring helps determine if operational and financial data collection and applications are accurately taking place.

SUMMARY

Pete and the rest of the team continued to gain insight into capacity management. They planned to continually improve the operational data and then the economic data. The team's vision was for IMAC to use capacity management as a competitive weapon. This meant the company would manage capacity using several model templates. Their vision included integrating the model into the product development process, the capacity authorization decision processes, the decision processes with suppliers and customer, and most importantly into the strategic decision making and planning processes.

Managing capacity better would increase IMAC's ability to provide products and services to their customers. It would also continue to create market opportunities and increase the pace of providing useful products and services to society for many years to come.

There was no doubt in the team's minds that manufacturing would be at the center of management's change process and that capacity management would be a critical component of manufacturing, operations, and strategy.

 | **The journey is now yours.**

GLOSSARY

Abandonment Elimination of idle or unneeded capacity.

Black Capacity Common color code for "Nonproductive Capacity" in black-and-white documents. See "Red Capacity."

Constraint 1. Bottleneck. 2. Limiting resource in a process. 3. Production center that has the highest traffic or intensity over a sustained period. 4. The constraint defines the global theoretical and global practical capacity.

Cost of Business 1. Capacity activities not required for production. 2. Idle capacity. 3. Business team responsibility.

Cost of Production 1. Capacity activities required for production. 2. Nonproduction and production capacity. 3. Manufacturing team responsibility.

Equipment Set 1. A machine. 2. A group of machines necessary to produce a product or complete a process.

Excess Capacity See "Idle Capacity."

Factory Balance 1. Capacity in production centers that is greater than the constraint. 2. Capacity equivalent of the traffic intensity delta to the constraint traffic intensity. 3. Also known as Factory Process Balance.

Global Theoretical Theoretical capacity identified by the constraint. See "Vertical Constraint Management."

Gray Capacity Common color code for "Idle Capacity" in black-and-white documents. See "Yellow Capacity."

Green Capacity Common color code for "Productive Capacity."

Idle Capacity 1. Formula: Marketable + Not marketable + Off-Limits. See formula terms. 2. Capacity not in use.

Local Optimization Practice of optimizing a subprocess that does not optimize the entire process.

Local Theoretical Theoretical capacity for a subprocess, for example, the theoretical capacity for a particular production center within a factory. Reference "Local Optimization."

Machine Capacity 1. Theoretical capacity for process analysis used in the capacity model. 2. Practical capacity used for planning.

Maintenance 1. A form of nonproductive capacity. 2. Work done to maintain or repair equipment sets or production center resources.

Marketable-Idle 1. Idle capacity for which a market exists. Causes for this idle capacity include competitor market share, product substitutes, and price constraints. 2. Direct responsibility of the business team.

Nonconstraint 1. A resource that is not a bottleneck. 2. A production center that has less traffic intensity than other resources over a sustained period. 3. Creates process balance capacity. 4. See "Constraint."

Nonproductive 1. States of capacity that exist for a given mix and volume but do not physically change the product. Examples include setups, waiting material due to material flow unbalance, maintenance, waiting operator, scrap, rework, and yield loss. 2. Variability.

Not marketable—Idle 1. Idle capacity for which a market does not exist, or a market exists but management has made a strategic decision to no longer participate in the market. 2. A target for abandonment, providing the cash flow NPV for abandonment is positive. 3. Responsibility of top management.

Off-Limits—Idle 1. Capacity that is neither available to the business team for external commitments nor available for abandonment. Examples include government holidays, management directives, and contractual agreements. 2. The responsibility of the business team.

Organization Responsibility Primary responsibility for a particular capacity activity. For example, design engineers are responsible for rework or process yield loss due to poor designs. Other responsibilities include these: marketing for marketable—idle; planning for variability due to actual production not aligned with planned production; finance for capital authorization rules that promote adding large capacity machines to increase factory balance; and management for accepting restrictions on legal workdays.

People Capacity 1. Scheduled capacity. 2. When scheduled capacity equals machine capacity (practical capacity), there is no marketable—idle capacity.

Practical Capacity 1. Maximum constraint capacity with historical or planned variability. This could be expressed in unit equivalents or in hours. 2. Formula: Nonproductive + Productive.

Production 1. Production results in the right product, of the right quality, in the right amount, at the right time, to the right customers. 2. Capacity used for physical change to the product. 3. In selected industries, where practice leads theory, product testing may be a production step, even though physical change does not happen.

Production Center One or more pieces of equipment with similar abilities in changing the product. Similar run rates or batch sizes do not require a unique production center.

Red Capacity Common color code for "Nonproductive Capacity."

Rework Product or material not manufactured to specifications that is subsequently reprocessed to achieve manufacturing specifications.

Scheduled Capacity 1. The capacity required to make the committed market demand. 2. Manned or people capacity. If manned capacity equaled practical capacity, idle capacity would be zero.

Scrap Product or material not manufactured to specifications that is subsequently either discarded or recycled in its original material forms.

SEMI E10 States of Equipment An industry-specific capacity model template. SEMI = Semiconductor Equipment and Materials International, a standard communication language for the semiconductor industry.

Setup 1 The cost of getting a process ready for a new production run. 2. A nonproductive use of capacity.

Slowdown The differential capacity of running the equipment, or process, at theoretical throughput rate compared to the actual throughput rate.

Theoretical 1. 24 hours a day, 7 days a week. 2. Expressed in units of time. Examples: a single unit production center with one machine would have a theoretical capacity rating of 24 hours. Two equivalent machines would have a rating of 48 hours. Two machines where one machine had a processing rate of 1.5 times the other machine would have a rating of 36 hours. Theoretical is a function of the production center and not a function of the product processing requirements. A 24-hour-rated machine that processes units that require 2 hours of processing has the same rated capacity as a 24-hour-rated machine that processes units that require 2 minutes of processing. 3. A useful measure for communicating opportunities. 4. Not a useful measure for making production commitments.

Variability 1. Factors in the process that hinder operational parameters, such as quality, process time, cycle time, yield, and output. These factors will increase cost. 2. Behavior in a process such as manufacturing that causes hindering effects.

Vertical Constraint Management The process of maximizing the constraint at different levels in the organization in a way that will optimize the business. Different levels include high-level business processes, order fulfillment, build, fabrication, and production center. There will be a constraint at each of these levels.

White Capacity Common color code for "Productive Capacity" in black-and-white documents. See "Green Capacity."

Yellow Capacity Common color code for "Idle Capacity."

Yield Loss 1. Material or products in a batch that are naturally lost as part of the process execution. 2. A process that has not developed enough to be repeatable.

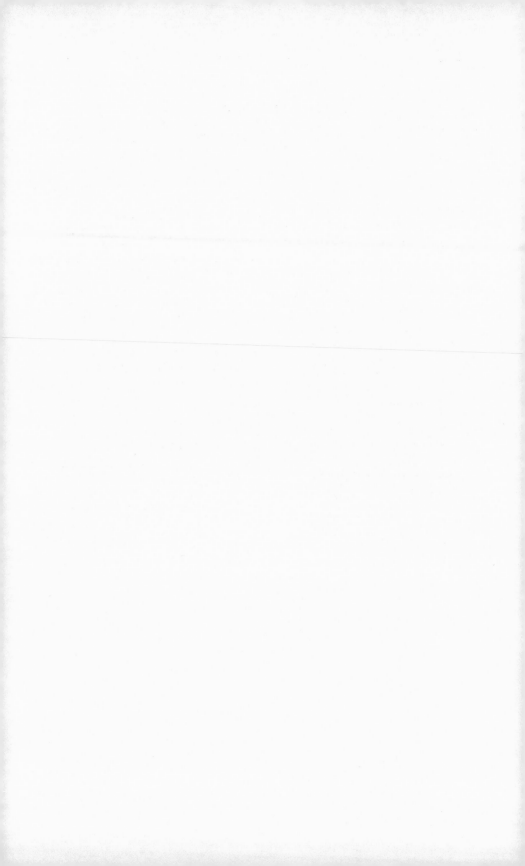

QUESTIONS & ANSWERS

This section answers several commonly asked questions about capacity and the capacity model. The first questions relate to implementation issues. Later questions clarify how we use certain classifications of activities in the model.

What cost should we use?

The capacity group recommends the use of the operating costs found in the operating financial statement. These are the costs most firms use to measure managers. These costs eventually roll up to senior management.

Exceptions to using operating costs exist. Examples include special analyses, such as those made for abandonment and investment decisions. During these analyses, cash flow is the preferred financial information source.

 | *Use the costs that are used to measure managers!*

What time period should we use?

The capacity model is a strategic tool. Quarters and years are the most useful periods. While the model may report for shorter periods, use care so that anomalies in operations, such as a machine being down for a week, do not distort the strategic picture of capacity.

What about depreciation and accruals?

The team building the capacity model must understand depreciation and other noncash items such as accruals, inventory change, and accounting reserves. Many rules behind these accounting methods are written for objectives that may not be consistent with economic realities in manufacturing and other processes.

When these accounting rules drive a significant distortion, there are several ways to put relevance back into capacity reporting. These include changing depreciation rules for factory accounting and making a "generally accepted accounting principles (GAAP)" adjustment at the business level. We could also record reserves and accruals only at the business level. One company identified the impact of financial accounting and dedicated one line item, called "balance sheet adjustment," for this reporting in the operating reports. The capacity model could follow this convention.

Off-line analysis may also show replacement values and realistic depreciation methods and lives. However, off-line analysis does not have the same behavior impact in the organization as the operating reports used to measure managers and report to the company's stockholders.

Since standby capacity for a nonconstraint tool is black or nonproductive capacity, will the focus on reducing nonproductive capacity encourage managers to keep equipment busy and build WIP?

First, since the model is a process model, white or productive capacity is computed from the output of the entire process. If increased WIP serves as a buffer and reduces nonproductive time in the constraint, white capacity increases. If increased WIP does not reduce nonproductive capacity, it may cause longer cycle times and increase many types of nonproductive capacity while reducing productive capacity.

Second, the model is a tool to use with good inventory policies. There are three primary rules driving required inventory levels. The first is the lead time driven by marketing strategies. The second is the inventory required to buffer the impact of variability on the constraint. This inventory supports maximum output at the lowest cycle time. The third is the business decision to store capacity as inventory, or to waste capacity in reduced work schedules. The model does not replace these reasons to hold inventory.

If the capacity model will provide the suggested benefits, why is the capacity model something new?

The model is not new. Its roots go back to the late 1800s and early 1900s, when manufacturing specialists like Frederick Taylor and H. L. Gantt focused management's attention on operations and activities causing variability and waste in the factory. Similar to many other manufacturing practices—such as just-in-time, process management, strategic supplier teaming, and focused factories—that were all practiced in the early 1900s, years of demand exceeding supply in the United States overshadowed the importance of these useful manufacturing practices.

Our factory and the mix we manufacture are different. How will this standard model apply to us?

The mix may be different, but there are also many similarities. These similarities include operational setups, conditional setups, pilot processing, quality procedures, preventive maintenance procedures, dummy processing, and batch sizes. Activities that are sources of nonproductive capacity provide learning opportunities, whatever the factory mix.

What is the process for identifying idle, gray, capacity?

Factory models can be a source for predicting idle capacity. Due to the infrequency and the wide distribution of many sources of variability, factory managers must validate model-generated idle capacity measures. We can track historical idle capacity and compare actual output by product to best-case output by product. In the end, the difference between practical capacity and scheduled capacity is idle capacity.

Idle time in a nonconstraint and subsequent yield loss are considered nonproductive. Since my area is not the constraint, I have no control over these activities. Why is my equipment area penalized for nonproductive capacity outside my control?

We measure the idle, nonproductive, and productive capacity by the entire output of the process. As a member of the operating team, part of your responsibility is focusing on throughput to sales. The model encourages global optimization, where everyone is working to optimize their process and the entire process.

How does the model relate to other initiatives, such as TPM and Cycle Time Reduction?

The model is a comprehensive 24-hours-a-day, 7-days-a-week, total-cost, closed-loop model. Accordingly, all management initiatives focused on excellence in operations can be monitored via the model. For example, if TPM reduces nonscheduled maintenance, this model would show how much capacity was converted from nonproductive to idle. If cycle time efforts reduced setup time or causes of variability, then the model would show a reduction of nonproductive capacity in those areas.

APPENDIX

Productive Capacity

A Measure of Value of an Industrial Property*

H. L. Gantt**
New York, NY

Some months ago a professor of political economy in one of our most conservative universities admitted to me that the economists had been obliged to modify many of their views since the outbreak of the European war. My comment was, that the professors of political economy were not the only people who had been obliged to modify their economic and industrial views.

The war has taught everybody something. Military methods have undergone radical changes, but industrial methods are undergoing changes which promise to be even more radical than the military developments have been.

---

*Presented at the Annual Meeting, December 1916, of The American Society of Mechanical Engineers
**Member of the Society
Reprinted with the permission of the American Society of Mechanical Engineers.

If there is any one thing which has been made clear by the war it is, that the most important asset which either a man or nation can have is the ABILITY TO DO THINGS. Our industrial and economic developments have in the past been largely based on the theory that the most important quality a man can possess is his *ability to buy things;* but the war has distinctly shown that this quality is secondary to the *ability to do things.* The recognition of this fact is having a most far-reaching effect, for it makes clear that the real assets of a nation are properly equipped industries and men trained to operate them efficiently. The money which has been spent on industrial property, whether it has been spent wisely or unwisely, and the amount of money needed to reproduce it are both secondary in importance to the *ability of that plant to accomplish the object for which it was constructed,* and hence cannot be given the first place in determining the value of the property.

Inasmuch as every industrial plant is built to produce some article of commerce at a cost which will enable it to compete with other producers, the value of a plant as a producing unit must depend upon its ability to accomplish the object for which it was created.

To determine the value of an industrial property, therefore, we must be able to know with accuracy the cost at which it can produce the product, and the amount it can produce. To compare two factories on this basis, their cost systems must be alike; for, if there is a lack of agreement as to methods of cost accounting, there will necessarily be a lack of agreement as to the estimated value of the properties. There are many methods of cost accounting; but there are only two leading theories as to what cost consists of. They are:

- First, that the cost of an article must include all of the expense incurred in producing it, whether such expense actually contributed to the desired end or not.
- Second, that the cost of an article should include only those expenses actually needed for its production, and any other expenses incurred by the producers for any reason whatever must be charged to some other account.

The first theory would charge the expense of maintaining in idleness that portion of a plant which was not in use to the cost of

EXHIBIT A–1

Idleness-Expense Chart

MILL, _____Textile_____ June, 19 96

Symbol	Department or Mach Class	% of Capacity used on Day Turn 10 20 30 40 50 60 70 80 90	Total Expense of Idleness	Lack of Work	Lack of Help	Lack of and Poor Material	Repairs	Poor Planning	Remarks
	Spinning		18 70	18 70					
	Winding		118 74		103 74		15 00		
	Doubling		10 61	10 61					
	Twisting		17 95	17 95					
	Quilling		20 67	10 67	10 00				
	Warping		390 75			390 75			Lack of Wound Yarn
	Weaving		915 25	75 00		840 25			Lack of Warps
	Finishing		210 72			210 72			Lack of Woven Goods
	Inspecting		49 70		10 70	39 00			Lack of Woven Goods
	Shipping		216 17	66 00		150 17			Lack of Woven Goods
	Total		1969 26	198 93	124 44	1630 89	15 00		

Approved By _____ SUPT.

the product made in that portion of the plant which was in operation; while the second theory would demand that such expense be a deduction from profits. When plants are operated at their full capacity, both theories give the same cost. When, however, they are operated at less than their full capacity, the expense of carrying the idle machinery is, under the first theory, included in the cost of the product, making the cost greater; while under the second theory, this expense of idle machinery is carried in a separate account and deducted from the profits, leaving the cost constant. It is most interesting to note that *when costs are figured on the second basis, great activity immediately ensues to determine why machinery is idle, and to see what can be done to put it in operation.* It is realized at once that this machinery had better be operated, even if no profits are obtained from its operation and only the expense, or even part of the expense, of maintaining that machinery is earned.

Exhibit A–1 illustrates this subject most clearly, and is an indication of the efficiency of the management as contrasted with that of the workmen, about which we hear so much. It is interesting to note that charts of this nature, which are being made monthly in several large plants, have already had a very educational influence on the managers of those plants. They show that idle machinery which cannot be used should be disposed of, and the money received, and the space occupied, put to some useful purpose.

A little consideration of the method of getting the data on this chart will make its value more apparent. It is a logical outgrowth of the paper I read at the Buffalo meeting on The Relation Between Production and Costs, and is based on the fact that simple ownership of a machine costs money, inasmuch as it takes away from available assets. For instance, if we buy a machine for $1,000 we lose the interest on that $1,000, say at 5 percent per year, then we have taxes on the machine at 2 percent and insurance of 1 percent. Further, the machine probably depreciates at a rate of 20 percent per year, and we must pay $50 or more per year for the rent of the space it occupies. All these expenses, together $330, go on whether we use the machine or not. Thus, the simple fact of our having bought this machine and kept it takes from our available assets approximately one dollar per day.

If now the cause for idleness is ascertained each day we can find the expense of each cause of idleness as shown on the chart. That part which is due to lack of orders points out that our selling policy is wrong, or that the plant is larger than it should be—in other words that somebody in building the plant has overestimated the demand. It is clear, however, that no conclusion should be based on the figures for one month, but on the results for a series of months during which the problem has been carefully studied. If a mistake has been made in building too large a plant, an effort should be made to determine the proper disposal, or utilization, of the excess, in order that the expense of idleness may be taken care of, even if no profit can be made.

The next column shows the expense due to a lack of help, which means that we must investigate the labor policy.

The next column showing the expense due to lack of, or poor, material, is an indication of the efficiency of the purchasing policy and storekeeping system. The next column reflects the repair and maintenance department.

If in any case the expense of idleness is greater than can be attributed to all of these causes together, it must go in the last column as poor planning.

We can hardly claim that such a chart gives us a *measure* of the efficiency with which the above functions are performed, but it certainly does give us an *indication* of that efficiency.

In several cases, the first of such charts gotten out resulted in the scrapping of machinery which had been idle for years. The space thus saved was used for a purpose for which the superintendent had felt he needed a new building.

In another case it resulted in the renting of temporarily idle machinery at a rate which went far toward covering the expense of carrying that machinery.

Under the first system of cost accounting the facts brought out by this method are not available and the increased cost that a reduced output must bear is a great source of confusion to the salesman. The newer system with its constant cost shows that nonproducing machinery is a handicap to the industry of a company, just as workmen who do not serve some useful purpose in a plant, or industry, are a handicap to that plant or industry. Similarly, plants or people, therefore, who do not serve some useful purpose to a community are a handicap to that community, for idle plants represent idle capital, and idle people are not producers but consumers only. The warring nations have recognized these facts, and put both idle plants and idle people to work whenever possible.

The statements so far made concern principally the operation of industrial plants and the production of articles of commerce; but they are none the less true concerning the construction of industrial plants.

We may ask the same question about construction that we ask about operation; for instance, should the cost of a railroad include all the money spent by the people engaged in building it, or should it include only such money as contributed to the building of the road? As an illustration, is the cost of a piece of road which was built and then abandoned for a superior route before being put into operation a part of the cost of the railroad built, or is it an expense due to improper judgment on the part of the builders?

I am not discussing the question as to whether the public should be called upon to pay interest on the money uselessly spent through improper judgment, but I do think that *in all construction it should be possible to separate those expenses which contributed to the desired result from those which did not so contribute.* A comparison of these amounts will give a measure of the efficiency of the builders. On this knowledge, proper action can ultimately be taken.

Still another factor enters into the value of a "going plant." We all have known cases where the same plant operated under one manager was a failure, and under another a very decided success. The value of a going plant, therefore, consists of two elements; namely, the value of the physical real estate and equipment, and the value of the organization operating it. In considering the value of an organization we should realize that it lies not so much in the personality of the managers or leaders (who may die or go elsewhere) as in the permanent results of their training and methods, which should go on with the business, and are therefore an asset and not an accident.

We have the authority of no less a person than Andrew Carnegie, Hon.Mem.Am.Soc.M.E., for the statement that his organizations were of more value to him than his plants. Before we can determine exactly the value of a going plant, therefore, we must find some means of measuring the value of the organization which operates it, for this is an integral factor in the valuation of an industrial property, which is just as real as the more tangible brick and mortar of which buildings are composed.

Our charts showing the expense of idleness give us at least a rough indication of this value, for they show the expense of inefficient management.

If the above premises are correct, the following factors are important elements in determining the value of an industrial property:

- The cost of the product.
- The capacity of the plant.
- The portion of the plant operated.
- The expense of maintenance of the idle portion.

———

In presenting his paper, the author said:

Inasmuch as the value of an industrial plant is measured by its ability to produce values, such a plant, which is not operated, has not actual but only potential value; actual value is conferred upon it only when human intelligence and industry are added to it to produce the results for which it was created. The fact that industrial plants are created in order to make some article which can be sold at profit or to render some service which can be sold at profit, amply justifies the statement that their value is dependent upon how they perform their functions. You may therefore divide the value of a going industrial property into two classes— that of the potential or static value of the plant itself, and that of the dynamic value of the organization operating it. In the past the former has been given attention by accountants almost to the entire exclusion of the latter, in spite of the fact that the stock-market prices and sales values of plants actually, though indirectly, reflect both values combined. If we would get a clear conception of the value of a going plant, we must find the means of measuring the value of the operating organization, which has often far more to do with its successful operation than the particular constructions and equipments of which it is composed.

In the operation of an industrial property it is seldom that all the expense incurred during any one month can be utilized to advantage; but if we can find how much was utilized and how well it was utilized, we can get some idea of the efficiency of the management. How well the money used was used, is indicated by the cost of the article produced; but there has, in general, been no indication as to what became of expense incurred, but not utilized. How much expense was incurred but not utilized, and why it was not utilized, are vital factors in any attempt to measure the efficiency of the management; hence it is to these questions that we give special attention in this paper.

At the Buffalo meeting last year I read a paper on the relation between production and cost, wherein I contended that the true cost should include only those items needed to produce the article, and that any other money expended while these articles were being produced, for any cause whatever, should be charged to some other account. People are pretty generally keeping an account of the money expended for producing articles. *In but few cases are they taking care to find out how much money was expended that did not produce anything.*

We are all familiar with the fact that machinery costs money, even when it is idle. Interest on the money invested, taxes, depreciation, insurance, etc., all go on whether the machinery is used or not. The value of a going plant is very materially influenced by the amount of the above items that are unused or unusable.

This is a factor which is directly in the control of the management, and does not in any way concern the inefficiency of the workman; but is a real factor in the valuation of a plant. Hence, a chart of the nature shown in my paper is a very real help in determining the value of a going plant.

DISCUSSION

W.S. Rogers thought that if Mr. Gantt's chart were real it would show the unbalanced condition of the plant, and that was just as important as anything. The divisions could be carried out further, and show plainly and clearly inefficiency, and the chart would point to and almost name the man, up in the higher office, who was killing himself at his desk, absolutely unable to go out and get a meal, and the biggest leak in the plant, knowing the least about it.

William W. Crosby, speaking of machine idleness, stated that in textile mills parts of looms would be in the storehouse for a whole year at a time. Looms would be put into operation at certain times because certain grades of cloth were demanded, but at other times they were not required. With a sufficiently worldwide market we could keep our mills running at somewhere near the capacity for which they were designed, but they could not be run fully and economically unless there were orders to run them on.

H.B. Cheney thought that every mill had some factor which, running on a particular product, was the controlling factor. In a cotton mill it was probably the looms. In making a chart such as Mr. Gantt had, the idleness portion of the chart should show, as he had arranged it, upon the 100 percent method. But when making calculations of cost, the controlling factor of the mill—the looms—should be taken into account, and all the departments which were necessary to supply the looms be considered as supply departments; if the looms ran 100 percent of the time, then 100 percent of all the expense of having that department supplied should be consumed in the cost; but if the looms, which were the controlling factor, only ran 85 percent, then only 85 percent of all the rest of the overhead should be consumed. All the departments having a chart on a 100 percent method would unquestionably bring out with the greatest clearness every point that was out of balance for that time. But it might be an entirely different matter six months later. Profits, he believed, instead of being figured on the article made, should be figured upon the running of the machines. In other words, one article might earn $1 a day profit on a loom, and another one $5 a day, and the former might make 50 percent profit and the latter but 10 percent.

H.M. Wilcox told of results secured at the Winchester Arms Company from a set of charts similar to Mr. Gantt's, only carried out in greater detail. They had studied the idle-machine time in the cartridge manufacturing department for a year or more, and determined how much time they were losing from the possible productive time of the machines due to tools, to machines, to labor and to excess equipment. This had directed their energy toward the points where they were weakest in eliminating the idle-machine time by giving their foremen specific information in regard to where time was being lost. The work became more interesting to the men without any effort other than pointing out where they were losing time, and a big gain in production was secured from the activities of the shop men themselves. The cost of scrap was added to the cost of the idle time and called the cost of lost effort, a report of which was given to the foremen weekly. The foremen had responded by attempting to reduce this waste, which was absolutely all waste as far as operating interests were concerned. Mr. Gantt's paper showed a way by which the efficiency of the management of an industrial plant could be measured periodically, and there seemed no very good reason why this should not be used as a basis for the extension of credit to that organization.

William Kent wrote that in a textile mill, if many different styles were made, the demand for which varied with the season and the fashion, part of the plant might be running full time and not be able to take the whole capacity of the remainder, some of which would therefore have to be idle part of the time.

The "expense actually needed" for the production of a variety of articles might thus include a part of the idle time of machines necessary to have on hand to care for a varying demand, but which could not be kept continuously employed; and in such a case it was right to charge some of the cost of idleness into the "normal burden" which was distributed in the machine-hour rate to the cost of the goods. A modification of Mr. Gantt's chart was thus suggested to show how much of the idleness of a machine or department was normal and necessary to the conduct of the business, and how much was abnormal and excessive. This might be done by drawing vertical lines on the percentage portion of the chart indicating the normal percentage of full capacity which each machine or department was expected to run during a month of good business. He thought the expression "value of the property" used in the paper was ambiguous and that its meaning should be defined.

John E. Mullaney stated that after his company had used Mr. Gantt's chart for about a year, he thought it might be worth while to know that if during the time they had been actually charging expenses to the operation they had been getting out their product at the fullest efficiency. In order to show this they had tried the idea of drawing a red line adjacent to each black line, the idea being to see if the black and red line agreed. If they did, the production in question had been made at 100 percent efficiency, that efficiency being based on the standards they had set for their production. The red ones which extended above the black were interesting to him, because they showed that they were getting a better productive efficiency out of these particular operations than they had previously planned. He thought this particular type of chart of working ideas could be applied to an industry in general, where each factory produced an article, and made its reports to some central head.

Willard C. Brinton stated that the discussion indicated some of the advantages which large businesses obtain from charting the figures relating to operation, sales and finance. A corporation doing a business of, say, $5,000,000 or more a year can ordinarily obtain a higher net-profit return from a graphic-control department than from any other way in which an equal amount of money can be expended. To get the best results from a graphic-controlled department a high-grade man should be in charge of the department, and this man should have no routine duties to prevent his giving the graphic charts all of the study which their importance justifies. Most large corporations having a national sales distribution required at least three thousand curves plotted continuously in order to properly control the business. To ensure that the man at the head of the graphic-control department might be free to report in an unbiased manner on the results of his studies of the charts, he should report directly to that officer of the company who was most actively guiding its affairs as a whole.

H.V.R. Scheel said that there had been presented for consideration a principle which was something more fundamental than a discussion of ways and means. That we now had a principle which was a definite measure of the efficiency of the management. Considerations of where responsibility lay had been broadened; the efficiency of the individual workman on a machine had become only a part of the efficiency of that whole for which the management, particularly, had to accept responsibility. In other words, Mr. Gantt's paper recorded a criticism of the management, but a constructive criticism, inasmuch as its form enabled the management to correct errors, modify plans and policies, and lay out a course of procedure more intelligent than any routine way of handling facts heretofore employed.

Keppele Hall wrote that he believed that most management engineers would agree that the vast majority of failures to succeed in business were due to the lack of what Mr. Gantt characterized as the "ability to do things" on the part of those really responsible, rather than to any other causes. One could well go a step further and state that in many instances a lack of real knowledge of the vital elements of operation precluded the exercise of this ability by those who really possessed it.

Harrington Emerson wrote that industrial property, according to the point of view, had three values: namely, the cost of its reproduction, the amount it would bring under the hammer, and its going value—the real value. This latter was difficult to determine, not because it was impossible on the basis of present or past returns and with due allowance for a definite amortization, to convert net income into capitalized value, but because no one could see into the future far enough to set either any real valid amortization or to determine what next year's profits would justify as increased value.

If of two plants one was able to operate materials, labor and capital valuation at standard, and each combination of materials, men and capital was yielding the largest margin between cost and sales price, while in the other plant operation was below standard and without reference to difference between cost and sales price, the first plant might very easily have many times the value of the second plant, although inventories were identical.

Edward W. Bemis thought that Mr. Gantt's paper did not have a large bearing on the work of the appraisal engineer in rate cases, for in these the attempt was to determine a fair value, which might be quite different from the value based on present rates and earnings. The productive efficiency should have some weight in rate cases; not, however, in determining the value of the property, but in leading commissions to allow a higher rate of return to a company of large productive efficiency, attributable to the excellence of the management, as compared with a business not so well managed.

Stuart W. Webb wrote that from the operating point of view Mr. Gantt's suggestions regarding idleness expense were highly important. It did not seem to him, however, that this item, which he had usually heard referred to as "load factor," reflected very accurately the value of the plant, due to the fact that so many different things might cause a low load factor. While most of them would probably be due to poor management, there would be other factors, such, for instance, as a distinct change in style (over which the management would have absolutely no control), which might throw a plant that had been operating efficiently entirely out of balance. It seemed to him, therefore, essential to add to the elements of which Mr. Gantt spoke at the end of his paper, "demand for the product and relations to the market (good will)."

Henry P. Kendall wrote that at the Plimpton Press that part of the burden which was not earned through the continuous operating of all or any of the machines, was called unearned burden. If the plant ran its full equipment full time, it had a credit; otherwise there was a certain amount of unearned burden, which was deducted from the profit and loss for each department at the end of every four weeks. He thought that if the net book value of a plant were based on the actual net investment and actual earnings after allowing a proper return on net investment, and costs were determined on a basis of direct expense with only the pro rata percent of burden applied regardless of whether the entire plant was operated or not, we would then have a common and standard way of determining these three points, which at the present time did not exist.

Robert B. Wolf said that he would like to call attention to the fact that Mr. Gantt had primarily made a strong plea for organization unity. The records exhibited formed a method of keeping track of the economic forces in the industry primarily for the purpose of enabling the management to have some record of their progress, but unless such records were furnished to the management they could not possibly use these forces intelligently. The management should be given the necessary information to enable those in charge to become efficient.

F.J. Cole wrote that one of the principal expenses in the production of manufactured articles resulted from not having on hand material in sufficient quantity or of proper quality. He showed that scheduling was most essential to anticipate correctly dates when things must be done in their proper sequence, and called attention to the fact that while all of the machines going all the time was the most economical way, a surplus of machines is sometimes required to take care of variations in product.

Arthur C. Jackson said that he hoped Mr. Gantt would eventually bring before and show the Society the necessity of charts for a whole industry, and select and define and portray on these charts the definite essentials for the economic operation of that industry, so that each member, each corporation within that industry, would have set up before it the beacons without which it would be very apt to run upon the rocks.

R.S. Hale wrote that many of the questions about cost and value would become simpler if we would give up the idea that there was any abstract "cost" or "value," and instead should work on the basis that the business of the accountant and engineer was to provide data which would make it easier for the executive to answer certain questions, or rather to enable the executive to take action.

Mr. Gantt's charts were exceedingly valuable, because they helped the executive to decide what he could have done if he had had more material, or if he had had more orders, or had had more help. Likewise they helped show what could be done if certain idle machinery were disposed of, etc. The cost figures they showed were, however, more than useless in some cases; but the same was true of all cost figures.

A.C. Jewett wrote that the expense of idle equipment shown by Mr. Gantt's chart must be combated, so far as idleness due to lack of orders was concerned, by an intense study of the sales problem. The engineer must direct the sales policies. He must direct the distribution of the products of industry. The consuming power of mankind was not limited. It was the distributing mechanism that was at fault when machinery in the mills and factories was idle and many people lacked sufficient food and clothing. This was not new, but it was new for the engineer to give serious attention to such matters as part of his work of industrial management.

J.B. Milliken wrote that his company defined the valuation of industrial property to mean the value at which the physical manufacturing property of a corporation was carried on its books. Mr. Gantt's paper evidently contemplated a different definition, viz., one including the efficiency of the plant, which involved the value of the organization operating it, which latter he stated "is an integral factor in the valuation of an industrial property." They agreed with Mr. Gantt, if by industrial property he meant all the values which were represented by the capital stock of a corporation, in which case the value of the management was reflected in the profit and loss account and in the market value of the corporation's shares; but the value of an organization could not properly be reflected in the physical assets of the corporation as shown by its books.

Their view was that the valuation of land, buildings and equipment should be shown on the books of a corporation at their original cost, less a depreciation for use or obsolescence. As a check on their valuations and depreciation ratios, they had appraisals made by professional appraisers at intervals of approximately ten years and compared results carefully with their valuations. They believed that appraisals should be made on the basis of present cost to replace, less proper allowance for age or for obsolescence, rather than on the basis of original cost, as the latter might be difficult to determine at the time of the appraisal and in some cases might represent more or less than real value, even at the time of purchase.

J.H. Williams wrote recommending the use of standard cost rates in cost accounting as a means of increasing efficiency of production, as well as Mr. Gantt's "constant" cost rates.

The use of standard cost rates, or rates representing what the cost should be as distinguished from what it was, made possible a daily comparison of the aggregate of the amount charged on the cost records (at standard rates) with the aggregate of the actual cost. Through their use it was possible to determine profit or loss due to *volume* daily; and by analysis of actual cost and comparison with standard cost, to determine their source.

On the other hand, through using the same standard rates in keeping production-cost records, it was also possible to determine profit or loss to *efficiency* daily by jobs as they were completed. By comparing the actual with the estimated cost of production, the operations involving profit or loss could be determined.

The Author. It is not pretended that my paper contains a complete solution of all our valuation or accounting problems, but it does point the way to detect many of the sources of waste and inefficiency which have heretofore been disregarded, and which cannot be detected until we get a proper appreciation of values.

Among the discussions which are particularly significant I may single out that of Mr. William Kent, who seems to be troubled about the difficulty of fixing a valuation for taxation purposes, if this method of valuation be accepted. This is particularly pleasing to me because, if the methods which are proposed did harmonize with the present system of taxation, I should feel very much discouraged, for there is nothing which is so detrimental to our industries and to prosperity in general as our system of taxation, by which the energy, initiative and business success of the individual are taxed for the benefit of the community, and the wealth created automatically by the community is allowed to go, without any return, to individuals who, as a rule, are contributing no equivalent return to that community. If the wealth created automatically by the community should be claimed by the community, it is highly probable that it would be unnecessary to tax any of the industrial activities of individuals, and Mr. Kent's troubles would absolutely vanish. If the proposed system of accounting has a tendency to make that fact clear, it will do much to lift a burden from our industries and enhance the prosperity of the workers.

If we would meet the competition with which some of us think we are so direly threatened after the war, we must encourage industry and discourage idleness, for the warring nations, having found what an enormous increase in strength such a procedure has given them, will hardly return, when the war is ended, to the other method which we seem to cherish so highly.

Arbitrary laws based on opinions inherited from a bygone age are not suited to an age like this, when the struggle for existence which is so keen in Europe threatens, perhaps in another form, to involve us; for the same causes that were active there are active here.

Ninety years ago Thomas Carlyle said, "the tools to the hands that can wield them."

It is a reversal of this policy which, more than all other causes combined, has brought Europe to such dire extremity. The control of the implements of production fell into the hands of investors, who saw more profit in the control of markets than in productive efficiency, which they did not understand.

Competition for the control of markets is at bottom the primary cause of the great war, and the fact that Germany had a somewhat clearer comprehension of the importance of productive efficiency and the necessity for the control of tools by the hands that can wield them is the explanation of her tremendous industrial and military power.

During the last eighteen months England has revised her policy, and through her Minister of Munitions has taken industrial control from stock and bond holders, and placed it in the hands of those who can "deliver the goods." The development she has made since this change is so phenomenal as to be almost unbelievable.

In her attempt to save her life she has learned that strength lies in productive efficiency. The other European nations have undoubtedly learned the same fact.

In the face of these examples are we still going to pin our faith to market control until aroused by a catastrophe, or can we learn from the fate of others and begin at once to develop productive efficiency? We have been talking efficiency in this country for over ten years, but so far the results have been lamentably small. This is not the fault of the workmen, for wherever we have had efficiency at the top we have had but little difficulty in training workmen to be efficient.

For years, with lack of efficiency at the top staring me in the face and hampering me at every turn, I have labored to find a means of measuring that efficiency, as it is perfectly evident that without efficient direction, efficient workmen are ineffective, even if it is possible to get them, which it usually is not.

If we can measure and evaluate the productive efficiency of the manager as we now measure that of the workman, we may hope for better results.

The only men organized for the promotion of productive efficiency are the engineers, and it is on your shoulders, gentlemen, that must fall the burden of showing what can be done.

I offer as a part of the work of measuring executive efficiency the chart shown in my paper. It is an attempt to measure the efficiency of the executives, and to indicate in a general way their value, which we know is an integral part of the value of any successful industrial property. This is only a first attempt, and I note that already one engineer has taken a step beyond what I offer.

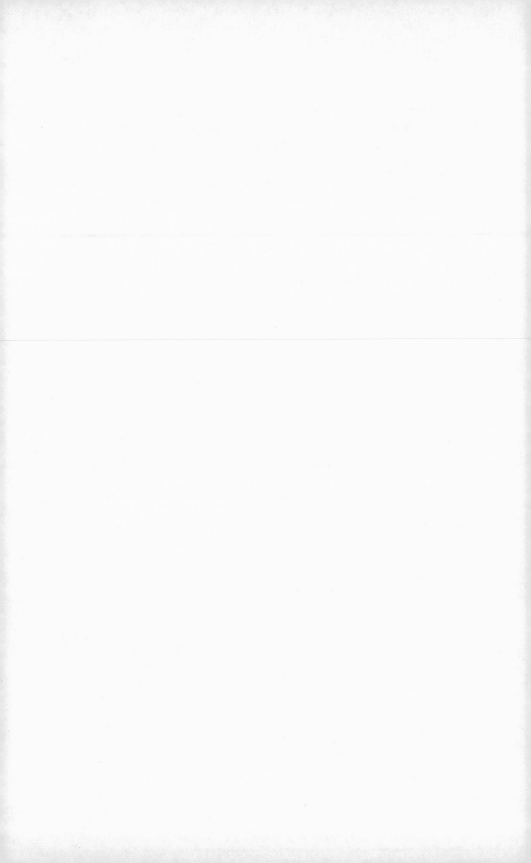

B

APPENDIX

The Relation between Production and Costs*

H. L. Gantt**

SYNOPSIS: *It has been common practice to make the product of a factory running at a portion of its capacity bear the whole expense of the factory. This has been long recognized by many to be illogical, but so far there has not been presented a rational theory as to what proportion of the expense such a product should bear. Mr. Gantt offers the theory that the amount of expense to be borne by the product should bear the same ratio to the total normal operating expense as the product in question bears to the normal product, and that the expense of maintaining the idle portion of the plant ready to run is a business expense not chargeable to the product made. This latter expense is really a deduction from profits, and shows that we may have a serious loss on account of having too much plant, as well as on account of not operating our plant economically.*

*Presented at the spring meeting, June, 1915, American Society of Mechanical Engineers.
**Consulting engineer, New York, NY.
Reprinted with the permission of the American Society of Mechanical Engineers.

Manufacturers in general recognize the vital importance of a knowledge of the cost of their product, yet but few of them have a cost system on which they are willing to rely under all conditions.

While it is possible to get quite accurately the amount of material and labor used directly in the production of an article, and several systems have been devised which accomplish this result, there does not yet seem to have been devised any system of distributing that portion of the expense known variously as indirect expense, burden or overhead, in such a manner as to make us have any real confidence that it has been done properly.

There are in common use several methods of distributing this expense. One is to distribute the total indirect expenses, including interest, taxes, insurance, etc., according to the direct labor. Another is to distribute a portion of this expense according to direct labor and a portion according to machine hours. Other methods distribute a certain amount of this expense on the material used, etc. Most of these methods contemplate the distribution of all of the indirect expense of the manufacturing plant, however much it may be, on the output produced, no matter how small it is.

If the factory is running at its full or normal capacity, this item of indirect expense per unit of product is usually small. If the factory is running at only a fraction of its capacity, say one-half, and turning out only one-half of its normal product, there is but little change in the total amount of this indirect expense, all of which must now be distributed over half as much product as previously, each unit of product thereby being obliged to bear approximately twice as much expense as previously.

When times are good and there is plenty of business, this method of accounting indicates that our costs are low; but when times become bad and business is slack, it indicates high costs due to the increased proportion of burden each unit has to bear. During good times, when there is a demand for all the product we can make, it is usually sold at a high price and the element of cost is not such an important factor. When business is dull, however, we cannot get such a high price for our product, and the question of how low a price we can afford to sell the product at is of vital importance. Our cost systems, as generally operated at present, show under such conditions that our costs are high and, if business is very bad, they usually show us a cost far greater than the amount we can get for the goods. In other words, our present systems of cost accounting go to pieces when they are most needed. This being the case, many of us have felt for a long time that there was something radically wrong with the present theories on the subject.

AN ILLUMINATING ILLUSTRATION

As an illustration, I may cite a case which recently came to my attention. A man found that his cost on a certain article was 30 cents. When he learned that he could buy it for 26 cents, he gave orders to stop manufacturing and to buy it, saying he did not understand how his competitor could sell at that price. He seemed to realize that there was a flaw somewhere, but he could not locate it. I then asked him what his expense consisted of. His reply was labor 10 cents, material 8 cents, and overhead 12 cents. My next question was: "Are you running your factory at full capacity?" and the reply was that he was running it at less than half of its capacity, possibly at one-third. The next question was: "What would be the overhead on this article if your factory were running full?" The reply was that it would be about 5 cents; hence the cost would only be 23 cents. The possibility that his competitor was running his factory full suggested itself at once as an explanation.

The next question that suggested itself was how the 12 cent overhead that was charged to this article would be paid if the article was bought. The obvious answer was that it would have to be distributed over the product still being made and would thereby increase its cost. In such a case it would probably be found that some other article was costing more than it could be bought for; and if the same policy were pursued, the second article should be bought, which would cause the remaining product to bear a still higher expense rate.

If this policy were carried to its logical conclusion, the manufacturer would be buying everything before long, and be obliged to give up manufacturing entirely.

The illustration that I have cited is not an isolated case, but is representative of the problems before a large class of manufacturers, who believe that all of the expense, however large, must be carried by the output produced, however small.

This theory of expense distribution is quite widespread and clearly indicates a policy that in dull times would, if followed logically, put many manufacturers out of business. In 1897, the plant of which I was superintendent was put out of business by just this kind of logic. It never started up again.

Fortunately for the country, American people as a whole will finally discard theories which conflict with common sense, and when their cost figures indicate an absurd conclusion, most of them will repudiate the figures. A cost system, however, that fails us when we need it most, is of but little value, and it is imperative for us to devise a theory of costs that will not fail us.

Most of the cost systems in use and the theories on which they are based have been devised by accountants for the benefit of financiers, whose aim has been to criticize the factory and to make it responsible for all the shortcomings of the business. In this they have succeeded admirably, largely because the methods used are not so devised as to enable the superintendent to present his side of the case.

Our theory of cost keeping is that one of its prime functions is to enable the superintendent to know whether or not he is doing the work he is responsible for as economically as possible, which function is ignored in the majority of the cost systems now in general use. Many accountants who make an attempt to show it are so long in getting their figures in shape that they are practically worthless for the purpose intended, the possibility of using them having passed.

In order to get a correct view of the subject we must look at the matter from a different and broader standpoint. The following illustration seems to put the subject in its true light:

Let us suppose that a manufacturer owns three identical plants of an economical operating size, manufacturing the same article— one in Albany, one in Buffalo and one in Chicago—and that they are all running at their normal capacity and managed equally well. The amount of indirect expense per unit of product would be substantially the same in each of these factories, as would be the total cost. Now, suppose that business suddenly falls of to one-third of its previous amount and that the manufacturer shuts down the plants in Albany and Buffalo and continues to run the one in Chicago exactly as it has been run before. The product from the Chicago plant would have the same cost that it previously had, but the expense of carrying two idle factories might be so great as to take all the profits out of the business; in other words, the profit made from the Chicago plant might be offset entirely by the loss made by the Albany and Buffalo plants.

If these plants, instead of being in different cities, were in the same city, a similar condition might also exist in which the expense of the two idle plants would be such a drain on the business that they would offset the profit made in the going plant.

Instead of considering these three factories to be in different parts of one city, they might be considered as being within the same yard, which would not change the conditions. Finally, we might consider that the walls between these factories were taken down and that the three factories were turned into one plant, the output of which had been reduced to one-third of its normal volume. Arguing as before, it would be proper to charge to this product only one-third of the indirect expense charged when the factory was running full.

A GENERAL PRINCIPLE

If the above argument is correct, we may state the following general principle: *The indirect expense chargeable to the output of a factory bears the same ratio to the indirect expense necessary to run the factory at normal capacity, as the output in question bears to the normal output of the factory.*

This theory of expense distribution, which was forced upon us by the abrupt change in conditions brought on by the war, explains many things which were inexplicable under the older theory and gives the manufacturer uniform costs as long as the methods of manufacture do not change.

Under this method of distributing expense there will be a certain amount of undistributed expense remaining whenever the factory runs below its normal capacity. A careful consideration of this item will show that it is not chargeable to the product made, but is a business expense incurred on account of our maintaining a certain portion of the factory idle, and chargeable to profit and loss. Many manufacturers have made money in a small plant, then built a large one and lost money for years afterward, without quite understanding how it happened. This method of figuring gives a clear explanation of that fact and warns us to do everything possible to increase the efficiency of the plant we have, rather than to increase its size.

This theory seems to give a satisfactory answer to all the questions of cost that I have been able to apply it to, and during the past few months I have laid it before a great many capable business men and accountants. Some admitted that this viewpoint would produce a very radical change in their business policy and are already preparing to carry out the new policy.

It explains clearly why some of our large combinations of manufacturing plants have not been as successful as was anticipated, and why the small but newer plant is able to compete successfully and make money, while the combinations are only just holding their own.

This idea so prevalent a few years ago, that in the industrial world money is the most powerful factor and that if we only had enough money nothing else would matter very much, is beginning to lose its force, for it is becoming clear that the size of a business is not so important as the policy by which it is directed. If we base our policy on the idea that the cost of an article can legitimately include only the expense necessarily incurred either directly or indirectly in producing it, we shall find that our costs are much lower than we thought and that we can do many things that under the old method of figuring appeared suicidal.

The view of costs so largely held, namely, that the product of a factory, however small, must bear the total expense, however large, is responsible for much of the confusion about costs and hence leads to unsound business policies.

If we accept the view that the article produced shall bear only that portion of the indirect expense needed to produce it, our costs will not only become lower, but relatively far more constant, for the most variable factor in the cost of an article under the usual system of accounting has been the overhead, which has varied almost inversely as the amount of the product. This item becomes substantially constant if the overhead is figured on the normal capacity of the plant.

Of course, a method of accounting does not diminish the expense, but it may show us where the expense properly belongs and give us a more correct understanding of our business.

In our illustration of the three factories, the cost in the Chicago factory remained constant, but the expense of supporting the Buffalo and Albany factories in idleness was a charge against the business and properly chargeable to profit and loss.

If we had loaded this expense on the product of the Chicago factory, the cost of the product would probably have been so great as to have prevented our selling it, and the total loss would have been greater still.

When the factories are distinctly separate, few people make such a mistake, but where a single factory is three times as large as is needed for the output, the error is frequently made, with results that are just as misleading.

DEFECT OF MAKING PRODUCT BEAR IMPROPER OVERHEAD EXPENSE

As a matter of fact it seems that the attempt to make a product bear the expense of plant not needed for its production is one of the most serious defects in our industrial system today, and farther reaching than the differences between employers and employees.

This problem that faces us is, then, first to find just what plant or part of a plant is needed to produce a given output, and to determine the overhead expense on operating that plant or portion of a plant. This is primarily the work of the manufacturer or engineer and only secondarily that of the accountant, who must, as far as costs are concerned, be the servant of the superintendent.

In the past, in almost all cost systems the amount of overhead to be charged to the product, when it did not include all the overhead, was more or less a matter of judgment. According to the theory now presented, it is not a matter of judgment, but can be determined with an accuracy depending upon the knowledge the manufacturer has of the business.

Following this line of thought, it should be possible for a manufacturer to calculate just what plant and equipment he ought to have and what the staff of officers and workmen should be to turn out a given profit.

If this can be correctly done the exact cost of a product can be predicted. Such a problem cannot be solved by a cost accountant of the usual type, but is primarily a problem for an engineer, whose knowledge of materials and processes is essential for its solution.

Having made an attempt to solve a problem of this type, one of the most important functions we need a cost system to perform is to keep the superintendent continually advised as to how nearly he is realizing the ideal set and to point out where the shortcomings are.

Many of us are accustomed to this viewpoint when we are treating individual operations singly, but few have as yet made an attempt to consider that this idea might be applied to a plant as a whole, except when the processes of manufacture are simple and the products few in number. When, however, the processes become numerous or complicated, the necessity for such a check becomes more urgent, and the cost keeper that performs this function becomes an integral part of the manufacturing system and acts for the superintendent, as an inspector, who keeps him advised at all times of the quality of his own work.

This conception of the duties of a cost keeper does not at all interfere with his supplying the financier with the information he needs, but insures that information shall be correct, for the cost keeper is continually making a comparison for the benefit of the superintendent, of what has been done with what should have been done. Costs are valuable only as comparisons, and comparisons are of little value unless we have a standard, which it is the function of the engineer to set.

Lack of reliable cost methods has, in the past, been responsible for much of the uncertainty so prevalent in our industrial policies; but with a definite and reliable cost method that enables us to differentiate between what is lost in manufacturing and what is lost in business, it will usually become easy to define clearly the proper business policy.

INDEX